World's Worst
Monsters
& Villains

World's Worst Monsters & Villains

KIERON CONNOLLY

www.scholastic.com

This edition published by Scholastic Inc., 557 Broadway, New York, NY 10012 by arrangement with Amber Books Ltd.

Scholastic Canada Ltd.
Markham, Ontario

Scholastic Australia Pty. Ltd
Gosford NSW

Scholastic New Zealand Ltd.
Greenmount, Auckland

1 2 3 4 5 6 7 8 9 10

ISBN: 978-0-545-47958-5

Editorial and design by
Amber Books Ltd
Bradley's Close
74–77 White Lion Street
London N1 9PF
United Kingdom
www.amberbooks.co.uk

Project Editor: Sarah Uttridge
Design: Keren Harragan

Printed in Shenzhen, China

Picture credits:
All illustrations by Myke Taylor, Colin Howard, Barry Croucher, Jean-Michel Girard and Terry Pastor/The Art Agency © Amber Books Ltd

Contents

Introduction 6

Mythical Monsters

Ghoul 8
Baba Yaga 10
The Elf King 12
Zmag Oghjeni Vuk 14
Troll 16
Nuckelavee 18
Amarok 20
Cockatrice 22
Kallikantzaros 24
Vetala 26
Tatzelwurm 28
Bunyip 30
Langsuir 32
Zahhak 34

Classic Folk Tales

The Giant from Sinbad's
	Third Voyage 36
The Sorcerer from Aladdin 38
The Wolf from The Three
	Little Pigs 40

The Giant from Jack and
	the Beanstalk 42
Lambton Worm 44
The Tanuki from
	Kachi-Kachi Yama 46
Little Otik 48
The Ogre from The Flea 50

Literary Monsters

Lord Voldemort 52
Gollum 54
Red Weed 56
Saruman 58
Tharks 60
The Snow Queen 62
Cthulhu 64

Gods & Monsters

Loki 66
Jormungand 68
Theelgeth 70

Set 72
Ammut 74
Humbaba 76
Gallu 78
Alecto 80
Vritra 82
Camazotz 84
Argos 86
Atraoimen 88
Morrigan 90
Xingtian 92
Xiang Yao 94

Index 96

Introduction

Do you know what scared people a thousand years ago? The same things that scare you. Cultures around the world have always told stories about monsters and villains. We may live in the frozen Arctic or the tropics, we may live in a city or a desert, but tales about serpents and giants, witches and wizards, wolves and demons are as popular today as they were in 1000 B.C.E.

In *World's Worst Monsters & Villains* we have collected 44 gruesome beasts from all over the globe and separated by thousands of years—the story of lion-faced giant Humbaba is almost 4,000 years old, while wicked wizard Voldemort from the Harry Potter books first appeared in the 1990s.

Some of these creatures, such as Gollum from *The Hobbit* or the wolf from "The Three Little Pigs," you may have heard of already. Others, like the camazotz bat-monsters or the skinless Scottish elf Nuckelavee, you probably won't have. But all of them are wonderful, scary characters from the world's best stories.

The book is divided into four chapters: characters from myth and folklore, like trolls, goblins, and ghouls; classic

fairy- and folk-tale characters, such as the giant
from "Jack and the Beanstalk"; characters from works
of fiction, such as Hans Christian Andersen's Snow
Queen; and finally characters from ancient myths about
the creation of the world.

In the chapters that follow, you will read about creatures that eat people and
husbands who mistakenly eat their wives, elves that steal children but children
who trick giants, serpents with nine human heads, and kings with snakes
growing out of their faces. And because these stories involve a certain
amount of death, you will also learn about the demons and gods who
guide people through the underworlds of the world's mythologies.

But it's not just ghoulish fun. If you've ever wondered how the ancient Chinese
explained why the sun sets in the west or how, according to the ancient Greeks,
the peacock acquired the distinctive "eyes" in its tail, you will find those questions
answered here, too.

The characters in these stories entertain us, educate us, and frighten us a little.
Exploring them helps us learn about more than 15 different cultures, including the
Inuit, Navajo, Mayan, Norse, Japanese, Chinese, Babylonian, Egyptian, Greek, and
Celtic. From vampires who ask riddles to headless giants who dance to boys who grow
out of tree stumps, this is a feast of beastly delights.

Ghoul

HEADDRESS
Coming from Bedouin stories, ghouls wear the typical headdress of people who live in the desert.

FACE
As undead spirits, ghouls have rotting faces that have become almost completely skeletal.

TONGUE
Living in the desert, the ghoul's dry tongue hangs out all day, thirsting for the human blood it will drink at night when it lures an innocent traveler or child away from the safety of their group.

BONE
Breaking into graves and feasting on the dead, this ghoul has been enjoying chewing on a human shin bone.

CLOTHES
Ghouls wear the clothes that they had when they were alive, but after so many years, these have now become ragged.

Ghouls live in the desert near burial grounds and although they look human, they can change into other animals, often hyenas. They rob graves, drink blood, steal coins, and eat human flesh, whether it is dead or alive. They are known to tempt travelers—especially children—into the desert, where they eat them. Often, they then take on the body of the person they have eaten. It is believed that ghouls are a type of genie whose father is Iblis, the devil in Islam. Ghouls are not intelligent, but they are strong and determined to eat. They come out at night and can be killed only by being burned.

ACTUAL SIZE

▶ SIDI NUMAN MARRIED A BEAUTIFUL WOMAN, Amine. Each day, she barely ate anything, usually just a bowl of rice. Sidi became suspicious when he realized that Amine left the house every evening. Following her one night, he discovered her beside a ghoul. They were both feeding on a corpse. At home the next evening, when Sidi confronted Amine, she cast a spell, turning him into a dog. A white witch made Sidi human again and turned Amine into a horse. Now that she was a horse, Sidi kept his wife in his stables.

Where in the world?

Stories of ghouls originate with Bedouin desert tribesmen in Arabia and date from the eighth century.

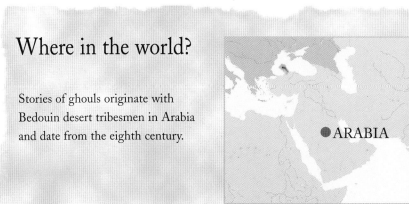

●ARABIA

Did you know?

• In the original Arabic tales, ghouls ate only people who were alive. They didn't rob graves or eat corpses.

• The earliest surviving written text about ghouls is in the collection *A Thousand and One Nights*, in which the story of Sidi Numan and Amine appears.

• The word ghoul is based on the Arabic *ghul*, meaning "demon." The star Algol comes from the Arabic *al-ghul*, meaning "the demon."

• In the Harry Potter novels, ghouls live in the homes of wizards and are noisy, but harmless. The Weasley family keeps a ghoul as a pet in their attic.

Baba Yaga

NOSE
Like an animal, Baba Yaga has an excellent sense of smell and can detect the presence of a stranger at a great distance.

CLAWS
Baba Yaga will tear strips of flesh from the backs of men she doesn't like. When chasing someone, she will use her claws to pull her way through trees and reeds.

MOUTH
Baba Yaga's mouth can grow so large that she can catch small children just by sticking out her tongue. Her teeth are made of iron and she can sharpen them.

NECKLACE
Baba Yaga is surrounded by death. Even her jewelry includes the teeth of dead people.

LEGS
One of Baba Yaga's nicknames is "Baba Yaga Bony Leg."

Like other witches, Baba Yaga rides through the air on a broomstick, but she's often perched in a kettle on top of the broom. She lives in a forest clearing in a house built on chicken legs that can move. Around her house are fences made of human bones and skulls with torches beaming through the eye sockets. Her house stands between the world of the everyday and the Otherworld. Her mouth can grow so enormous that it can be mistaken for a cave, and once people have entered she will eat them. She also controls the many-headed, fire-breathing dragon Chudo-Yudo. Sometimes she travels with Death.

ACTUAL SIZE

▶ AN ELDERLY COUPLE HAD A DAUGHTER but couldn't find a godmother for her. Baba Yaga, dressed as an old woman, offered to be godmother and took the girl to live with her. But as soon as the girl made a little mistake, Baba Yaga threw her out. Lost in the forest, the girl met a prince, who married her. Together, they had three sons, but Baba Yaga snatched back the girl and took the boys as payment for the girl's mistake. The prince followed, but Baba Yaga would release only the boys, keeping the girl to serve her.

Where in the world?

The folk legend of Baba Yaga is known throughout Russia and Eastern Europe. She is said sometimes to be seen flying on a mortar and pestle.

●RUSSIA

Did you know?

● Although usually an evil character, Baba Yaga can be good. If people are in difficulties, she can offer them a mirror, a ring, or a sword that will help them with their problem.

● It is said that Baba Yaga controls the flow of milk from a cow, when rain falls, and how well crops grow. She can also eat the sun or moon.

● Koshei the Deathless is a man who sometimes appears as a dragon. Baba Yaga makes him immortal by placing his soul outside his body hidden in an egg. Finally, though, a prince finds the egg and kills Koshei.

● Baba Yaga has invisible servants in her house. However, anyone who dares ask about these servants is killed.

The Elf King

CROWN
The elf king wears a crown and presents himself as a sophisticated elf gentleman.

MOUTH
The elf king speaks sweetly to the adults and children he tries to steal. But his words cannot disguise his evil nature and his ugliness.

ARMS
The elf king tries charm and persuasion at first, but if those fail he uses his strong arms to drag his victim into the darkest corners of the forest.

CLOTHES
Only the person whom the elf king is trying to lure away can see the elf king. Other people can see only the trees or mist rising in the forest.

TAIL
Descriptions about the elf king vary, but in many versions of the story he has a tail.

The elf king is a supernatural being said to live in the forests of Scandinavia and Germany. He has a tail and wears a crown. When people are journeying through the forests at night, the elf king tempts them with a life of wealth and comfort if they will join him.

ACTUAL SIZE

To women he offers his love and to men he offers his daughters, who sing and dance. People must resist his tempting offers, or the elf king will steal their souls and kill them. Sometimes, even if the human has resisted temptation, the elf king will take their life by force.

▶ A FATHER WITH HIS SICK CHILD IS RACING ON HORSEBACK through the forest at night. The boy is scared because he can see the elf king calling out to him. His father says it's just a wisp of fog. The elf king speaks to the boy, tempting him with riches and his daughters. The boy calls out again to his father, but his father says it's just the trees moving. This time, the elf king attacks the boy and he cries out. At last, the father reaches a safe farmyard, but his son is dead.

Where in the world?

The legend of the elf king comes from Denmark, but it is popular across Scandinavia and in Germany.

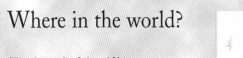

● DENMARK

Did you know?

• The most famous version of the legend of the elf king is found in the German poem "Der Erlkönig" (1782) by Johann Wolfgang von Goethe. In 1821, Franz Schubert set the poem to music in a song.

• According to the legend, elves live by burial mounds.

• In Scandinavian versions of the story, it is elf maidens and the elf king's daughters who tempt the travelers, not the elf king himself.

• In a Danish version of the legend, Sir Oluf is riding through the forest to his wedding. An elf maiden invites him to dance with her and to enjoy her gifts and gold. When he refuses her offers, she hits him and sends him on his way. He reaches his castle, but the following morning his bride finds him dead.

Zmag Oghjeni Vuk

MOUTH
Zmag Oghjeni Vuk was a
rare example of a fire-
breathing werewolf dragon.
He didn't target ordinary
people, but attacked enemy
soldiers in battle instead.

WINGS
When Zmag changed from
a normal military leader into
a werewolf, he also grew
dragon's wings. With these,
he could fly high enough to
glide over enemy soldiers.

HIND LEGS
Zmag could run very fast, using his
flapping wings to help him. He was
known to chase away terrified enemy
armies, with blue fire bursting from
his mouth.

PAWS
As a human child, Zmag once had a
birthmark of a wolf's paw and a sword
on his lower leg.

Zmag Oghjeni Vuk was a Balkan werewolf that was not only born a normal man but was a real historical figure, Vuk Grgurević Branković, a great Serbian military leader of the late fifteenth century. He was so brave in battle that legends built up around him and he was given the nickname "Fiery Dragon." Because his name "Vuk" already meant "wolf," the legend grew. It was said he was born with a birthmark the shape of a saber sword and a wolf's paw, that he was the son of a fiery dragon, and that he himself could breathe fire so hot that it was blue.

ACTUAL SIZE

▶ BRANKOVIĆ AND HIS SOLDIERS FOUGHT THE TURKS ALL DAY. As the sun began to set, Branković found himself on the castle ramparts with six Turks advancing toward him on either side. At that moment, hair and dragon's wings burst through his armor, he grew taller, and fire shot from his mouth, burning the first two Turks. He quickly defeated all the Turks on one side and when he turned around, the other Turks had fled. After the battle, snakes brought him herbs, fairies nursed his scratches, and wolves licked his wounds clean.

Where in the world?

Vojvodina, Serbia, in the Balkans in southeastern Europe. Vuk Grgurević Branković also fought battles against the Czechs, Poles, and Austrians.

● BALKANS

Did you know?

● Vuk Grgurević Branković became a legendary hero in the Serbian epic poems that were written after his death.

● In some versions of the legend, when he transformed into a werewolf he had eagle's wings and dragons under his armpits. Unlike other werewolves, he could choose if he wanted to turn into a werewolf at night.

● In Russia in the eleventh century, there was a real prince and warrior named Prince Vseslav of Polotsk. According to folklore, he turned into a werewolf, too.

● The usual name for a werewolf-vampire in Serbia is *vukodlak*, which means "wolf's hair." The creature sleeps in its grave with its eyes open, and its hair and nails grow to extreme lengths. When there is a full moon, it attacks men and drinks their blood.

Troll

EYES
Trolls have good vision and magic powers at night, but exposure to sunlight turns them into stone.

MOUTH
Some trolls are man-eaters. They can be evil and very stupid, but still strong and determined enough to kidnap children and rampage through a house.

SKIN
A troll's hide is very tough and will not cut easily. In J.R.R. Tolkien's novel *The Hobbit,* a troll is attacked with a sword. The sword is damaged, but the troll remains unhurt. Trolls also have black blood.

ARMS
Not being converted to Christianity, trolls are believed to have destroyed churches under construction by throwing whole boulders at them.

From Norse folklore, trolls are elves, both male and female, who live in their own family groups in the mountains and away from people. Exposure to sunlight turns them into stone, but at night they have magic powers. Some eat men, they are known to kidnap children, and they attack farms. Trolls are scared of lightning and the sound of church bells will force them to move away eventually. For centuries, it was customary to leave food outside of your house for the trolls to stop them from attacking it. Standing stones are often said to be either a troll turned into stone or a stone thrown by a troll.

ACTUAL SIZE

▶ ONE CHRISTMASTIME, HEDINN WAS IN THE FOREST when he saw a troll woman riding on a wolf with snakes for bridles. She asked him to join her, but when he wouldn't she put a curse on him. At Christmas dinner, the curse made him vow to take his brother's wife. Later, Hedinn's brother Helgi was challenged to a duel. During the duel, Helgi received a deadly wound because of the troll woman's curse. Dying, Helgi called for his wife and gave his blessing for his brother to marry her.

Where in the world?

Across all Scandinavia. The fiercest trolls are said to be found in Norway, while the trolls that are tricksters are found in Denmark.

SCANDINAVIA

Did you know?

• Some trolls have two or three heads.

• In the Norwegian folk tale "Per Gynt," Per is a hunter who rescues three dairy maids from trolls and shoots the gigantic, worm-shaped troll Böyg. In a scene in Henrik Ibsen's play *Peer Gynt,* the trolls offer to poke out Peer's eyes, so that he does not have to see how ugly the troll princess is whom he is about to marry.

• In J.R.R. Tolkien's novel *The Hobbit,* the wizard Gandalf has to rescue the hobbit, Bilbo Baggins, from trolls.

• Trolls are often believed to live in burial mounds. Some are the same height as humans, but others are smaller. A sorcerer has the power to turn someone into an ugly troll.

Nuckelavee

EYE
Nuckelavee has a single eye that burns bright with a flame.

MOUTH
Nuckelavee's mouth is ten times larger than a human's.

BODY
Nuckelavee is sometimes described as skinless and half elf, half horse. At other times, he is seen as an elf riding a horse. Similar to Nuckelavee, the horse is also skinless.

BODY
Nuckelavee is skinless and his flesh raw, so his blood can be seen pulsing through his veins. All his sinews are visible, too.

FEET
Living in the sea, Nuckelavee has webbed feet. Although he loves seawater, on land he hates freshwater and runs away from it.

Nuckelavee is a gruesome sea monster and, unusually, one of the few sea monsters who attacks on land. The breath of this skinless beast can kill children and farm animals and ruin crops. Being from the sea, he is used to salty seawater. He does not like freshwater and is unable to cross rivers or streams or enter lochs (lakes).

ACTUAL SIZE

He is never seen on dry land when it's raining, so droughts are blamed on Nuckelavee. He hates the smell of burning seaweed and if he sees anybody doing it, he flies into a rage, bringing plague, killing cattle, and poisoning the fields.

▶ A BOY WAS OUT WALKING WHEN HE SAW NUCKELAVEE on a huge horse. Nuckelavee began chasing him and the boy found himself beside a loch. He splashed Nuckelavee's horse, which, hating freshwater, reared back. But the boy couldn't jump in the loch because there might have been kelpie (water spirits) in it. He began running and saw a stream up ahead. He raced to the stream and just as Nuckelavee tried to bite him, he jumped across. Nuckelavee couldn't cross the running water and so the boy was safe.

Where in the world?

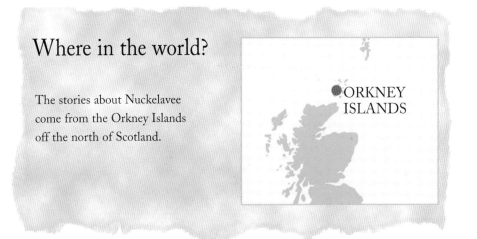

The stories about Nuckelavee come from the Orkney Islands off the north of Scotland.

● ORKNEY ISLANDS

Did you know?

● Sometimes Nuckelavee is seen on a horse and it almost seems as if he is part monster, part horse. In this way, he is similar to the water-horse of Scots and Scandinavian folklore. Water-horses would tempt children into riding on their backs, before diving into the sea and drowning the children.

● Nuckelavee hated the smoke that came from burning seaweed, but starting in the eighteenth century onward, people in the Orkneys burned seaweed to make kelp, from which they could make salt.

● Nuckelavee was most recently reported seen on the islands of Hoy and Sanday in the Orkneys.

● On the Shetland Islands off northern Scotland, Nuckelavee is called Mukkelevi and is known as a sea devil. In Scandinavia, water-horses are called *nøkk*.

Amarok

HEAD
The amarok is a wolf, but is far, far bigger than wolves we know. Its head is at least twice the size of a gray wolf.

NOSE
Even in the most frozen days of winter, the sensitive nose of the amarok can follow the scent of humans.

EARS
Extra-sensitive hearing enables the amarok to hear things many miles away. It can detect a caribou or a human settlement from a great distance, and then hunts them down.

LEGS
The amarok can leap great distances to pounce on its prey. An excellent hunter, it can move almost silently to surprise people or animals.

PAWS
An amarok can easily tear apart the flesh of its prey with its claws.

Wolves hunt in packs, but the gigantic amarok wolf from the Inuit mythology of northern Canada and Greenland hunts alone. Unlike the arctic wolf, the amarok will attack humans, especially anyone foolish enough to hunt alone at night. And once attacked, they will be eaten. Also, while the arctic wolf relies on stamina to run for longer—rather than faster—than its prey, the amarok easily outruns caribou, musk oxen, and, certainly, humans. Once the amarok has picked up your scent or seen you, just hope that it isn't hungry or angry, or pray that a tastier caribou turns up for the amarok to devour instead of you.

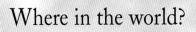
ACTUAL SIZE

▶ THE BOY WAITED UNTIL DARK AND THEN CREPT OUT. He had been told that he was too young to hunt caribou, but he thought that if he caught one on his own, his family would be very impressed. In the darkness, he heard a scratching sound and thought that it was a caribou looking for grass. The boy lit a match, but what he saw made him drop it instantly—in front of him stood the largest wolf he'd ever seen. Its eyes were glaring and it bared its fangs. The wolf pounced and in the darkness the boy cried out.

Where in the world?

Among the Inuit people in northern Canada and Greenland. Amarok means wolf in Inuktitut, one of the Inuit languages.

CANADA

Did you know?

• When a caribou herd grows too big, food becomes scarce and the animals grow weak and get sick. According to some legends, it is at this point that the amarok preys on the weakest. However, fewer caribou mean more food for the remaining animals to eat and grow strong again.

• It is possible that the amarok is based on the folk memory among the Inuit people of the dire wolf or the hyaenodon (an ancestor of the hyena), both of which are now long extinct.

• Other Inuit mythical beasts are the Tornits, which are similar to the Bigfoot or Yeti myth of a giant hairy man. Tizheruk, a snakelike monster, is another creature of Inuit mythology.

• In winter, the Inuit gather in a *qagip* (a giant snow house) and on summer evenings, they meet outside to share stories, such as folk tales about amarok.

Cockatrice

WINGS
The cockatrice has wings like a dragon's. These enable it to fly up and then land on a victim's back or head to attack them.

EYES
Beware of the gaze of the cockatrice. Even when it is dead, it can turn you into stone if you look it in the eye.

BEAK
The cockatrice's beak can snap off fingers and break necks with a single bite.

MOUTH
The "Cock-a-doodle-do!" of a rooster is usually a pleasant farmyard call, but the shriek of the cockatrice is alarming and bone-chilling. Upon hearing it, farmers stop what they're doing, parents rush their children into their homes, and soldiers reach for their weapons.

Even dead, the cockatrice can turn someone into stone. Never, ever look one in the eye, even after its head has been cut off and it is no longer breathing. The weasel is the only animal that will not be turned into stone if it looks the cockatrice in the eye, touches a cockatrice, or is breathed on by a cockatrice. The cockatrice has similarities with the basilisk, but the basilisk has a serpent's body instead of a dragon's body. The cockatrice was born in an egg laid by a rooster, which was then hatched by a toad.

ACTUAL SIZE

▶ IN THE ENGLISH VILLAGE OF WHERWELL, there once lived a cockatrice that terrorized the villagers. Finally, they managed to imprison the cockatrice in the dungeons below Wherwell Priory. They offered a reward to anyone who could kill the cockatrice. No one was successful until a man called Green lowered a mirror into the dungeon. The cockatrice exhausted itself battling its reflection in the mirror. With the cockatrice weakened, Green was able to go into the dungeon and kill it. For many years, a weather vane in the shape of a cockatrice perched on the village church.

Where in the world?

The best known story tells of a cockatrice in Wherwell, Hampshire, in southern England, but they are known across Europe.

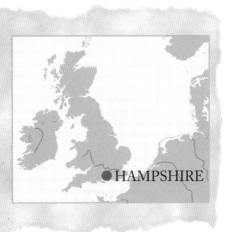

●HAMPSHIRE

Did you know?

• In some versions of the cockatrice legend, the cockatrice had two human heads with the second one at the end of its tail.

• Another myth said that the cockatrice would die if it heard a rooster crow and that the only antidote for its poison was to carry a cockerel.

• The cockatrice appeared in European mythology in the twelfth century and was a popular character until the seventeenth century. Today, statues of the cockatrice still exist. One can be seen above a doorway at Belvedere Castle in Central Park, New York City.

• The cockatrice is similar to the ancient Greek mythical witch Medusa, whose gaze could turn a person into stone. Sometimes the cockatrice doesn't turn people into stone—it just kills them.

Kallikantzaros

BRAIN
They can be very fierce and nasty, but kallikantzaros aren't very clever. They cannot count to three and can easily be distracted by riddles and games.

ARMS
The kallikantzaros are very strong and good at climbing onto roofs, breaking into bedroom windows, or climbing down chimneys. To stop them from entering your house, always keep the fire lit in the grate.

BODY ODOR
They smell disgusting, but they force humans to hold them and dance with them until the humans drop down dead.

SKIN
They are allergic to light and have to hide from the sun during the day.

FEET
On their feet, the kallikantzaros have cloven hooves like deer or sheep.

All year long the kallikantzaros goblins work underground, trying to chop down the World Tree that supports the Earth. Just before they succeed, Christmas arrives and they hurry up to the surface to cause mischief for two weeks. These grotesque, foul-smelling goblins make travelers dance with them until the traveler drops dead of exhaustion. Then, they eat them. They also kidnap women, destroy crops,

kill livestock, and knock down houses. They come out only at night and are allergic to sunlight. They can be stopped by clever riddles (they can't count to three). Keeping a fire lit in the fireplace stops them from coming down the chimney.

ACTUAL SIZE

▶ WHEN THE KALLIKANTZAROS THREATEN TO EAT BEAUTIFUL KALLO, she says: "You can't eat me in my old dress." So the goblins steal a fine dress for her. Then, she says she needs a coat, and again the goblins hurry off to find her a coat, followed by an umbrella, a comb, face powder, and other presents. She keeps the goblins busy all night and by dawn they have run out of time to eat her. She leaves with presents, which makes her lazy, jealous sister, Marbo, even more jealous than before.

Where in the world?

Kallikantzaros can be found under the ground all over Greece.

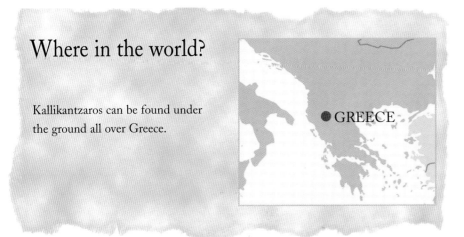

● GREECE

Did you know?

● When the kallikantzaros return to the underworld, they start to chop down the World Tree again. They almost succeed by the next Christmas, when they must stop to head up to the surface.

● The word kallikantzaros might come from "kalos-kentauros," which means "beautiful centaur."

● According to legend, when children born during the twelve days of Christmas grow to adulthood they will be in danger of becoming a kallikantzaro each Christmas. This can be prevented, however, by wrapping the newborn baby in garlic leaves or straw.

● In the folk tale "Kallo and the Goblins," Kallo's jealous, ugly sister Marbo goes to see the goblins, but they don't give her any presents and instead scratch her face. Marbo is rescued and Kallo uses the face powder the goblins gave her to heal her sister.

Vetala

FEET
Like a bat, the vetala used its feet to cling to branches as it hung upside down from trees. It was only ever seen in graveyards at night.

BRAIN
The vetala existed between the worlds of the living and the dead. That way it knew a great deal about the past, present, and future.

EYES
Just by looking at them, the vetala could put a curse on a person, driving them insane, or put a curse on a field, ruining its crops.

CLOTHES
The vetala wore a strange combination of clothes and jewelry taken from some of the dead bodies the vetala had possessed.

VOICE
The vetala was always laughing at people and telling stories, even when they cut it out of its tree.

In Hindu folklore, the vetala is an evil spirit that haunts burial grounds. It exists between the world of the living and the dead. It can take possession of a corpse, turning it into a vampire. It can also drive people insane, kill children, and ruin crops. It is neither alive nor dead, so it knows a great deal about the past, present, and future. Sorcerers often try to capture it and make it a slave. Saying prayers when in a graveyard can keep the vetala away. Performing a funeral for the vetala can free it from its curse.

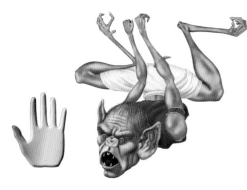

ACTUAL SIZE

▶ A SORCERER ASKED KING VIKRAM TO CATCH A VETALA that hung from a tree in the middle of a burial ground. The only way to do this was by keeping silent, but every time Vikram caught the vetala, it would ask the king a riddle. The vetala promised that if the king couldn't answer the riddle, the vetala would allow itself to be captured. But each time the king was asked a riddle, he couldn't resist giving the correct answer. When that happened, of course, the vetala escaped back into its tree.

Where in the world?

The vetala tricked the legendary King Vikram in Ujjain, Madhya Pradesh, India in the first century B.C.E.

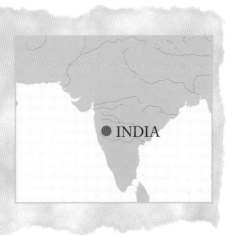

● INDIA

Did you know?

• The vetala first appeared in a collection of folk tales dating from the eleventh century called the *Baital Pachisi*. But stories about vetala are probably even older.

• On the twenty fifth time that King Vikram heard a riddle from the vetala, he didn't know the answer and so the vetala allowed itself to be captured.

• The vetala can also be a force for good. In the story of King Vikram and the vetala, the vetala tells the king how the sorcerer is planning to kill him. The king then manages to kill the sorcerer first by the same method!

• Victims brought back to life by the vetala always have their hands and feet pointing backward. It is thought that vetala are the spirits of people whose families didn't give them proper funerals.

Tatzelwurm

HEAD
One of the most unusual beasts to look at, the tatzelwurm has the head of a cat and a body like a lizard or an amphibian but covered with scaly skin.

MOUTH
The fumes from the tatzelwurm's mouth are so poisonous that they can kill people.

CLAWS
The tatzelwurm has long, ferociously sharp claws that it uses to dig its way under rocks and into hollows, where it lives.

FEET
In some sightings, the tatzelwurm is described as having four legs and dragging its snakelike tail behind it. On four legs or two, it can leap great distances to attack people.

A legendary creature from the European Alps, the tatzelwurm, which means "claw worm," is able to defend itself by hissing lethal fumes. It is more likely seen during dry periods and droughts. The tatzelwurm steals cows' milk and can jump 9 feet (2.75 m) to attack farm animals, children, and travelers. It lives under rocks, in hollows, and in holes dug by other animals. It is rarely seen, though reports of sightings (and bitings) date back to the eighteenth century. Some people think that it is a kind of dragon, but it has never been caught to be properly identified.

ACTUAL SIZE

▶ THE BOY WAS HIDING BY THE RIVERBANK to catch a glimpse of the animal that had been killing the snakes when he heard a hissing behind him. He turned around and was horrified to see an animal with the head of a cat, scales of a fish, and the long body of a giant worm. The tatzelwurm hissed again—its breath was so disgusting the boy almost fainted. The tatzelwurm leapt toward the boy, but he jabbed it with his stick. The tatzelwurm's blood burst onto the boy's leg, burning his skin, and the boy fled for his life.

Where in the world?

Most recently spotted in Tresivio, in the Italian Alps, but the tatzelwurm has been reported in the Swiss and Austrian Alps, too.

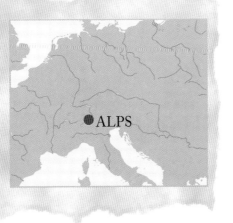

●ALPS

Did you know?

• Disbelievers say that the tatzelwurm is just a salamander (an amphibian) or a relative of the Gila monster lizard (a reptile), which is venomous and lives in burrows at high altitudes.

• Other names for the tatzelwurm are *Stollenworm* (tunnel worm), *Bergstutzen* (mountain stump), and *Springwurm* (jumping worm). The French name is *arassas* and the Italian name is *basilisco*.

• The first recorded sighting of the tatzelwurm was in 1779. An Austrian farmer found two tatzelwurms attacking his livestock. One of the creatures jumped at the farmer, who suffered a heart attack. He lived just long enough to tell his family what he'd seen.

• In 1954, a Swiss photographer presented what he claimed was a photograph of a tatzelwurm. However, the photograph showed a dead-looking, unconvincing creature and people dismissed it as a hoax.

Bunyip

HAIR
The bunyip is completely covered from head to foot in long green hair. It was once an ordinary man, but he offended the gods, so they turned him into the bunyip.

TEETH
Needle-sharp teeth enable the bunyip to tear up and eat whatever water creatures it finds. If a human is unlucky enough to come within its reach, the bunyip will bite the neck and then eat the victim.

LEGS
Underneath all of the hair are two legs. Other reports of bunyip sightings say that it walks on four legs. All agree that it can leap out of the swamp at great speed.

CAMOUFLAGE
Like a crocodile, the bunyip lies just below the surface of a river, looking very much like water weeds. But anyone dipping a foot in the water will receive a sharp shock.

There are many different descriptions of bunyips, but in each the beast is a huge, evil creature that lives in swamps, lakes, and riverbeds and, unseen, can be recognized by its loud cry. It hates humans and will eat one if it feels its home is under threat—it also creeps up on people at night. When a group of young women tried to test the bunyip, it made them its water-spirit slaves. These women now live in the swamps and, using their beautiful singing voices, tempt men to join them. According to legend, the bunyip was once a man, but after insulting the gods he was turned into a bunyip and banished.

ACTUAL SIZE

► GOONDAH WENT FISHING AND CAUGHT A BUNYIP CUB. His friends told him to throw it back, but Goondah had promised his girlfriend that he'd bring her some meat. He ran to take the cub to his girlfriend, but behind him the mother bunyip was crying out and making the waters rise higher. Goondah and his girlfriend had to climb a gum tree to escape the waters, but still the waters kept rising. As Goondah looked down, he realized that his feet had changed—the bunyip had turned him and his girlfriend into black swans.

Where in the world?

Bunyips originate with the Wemba Aborigines in southeastern Australia, but they are part of Aboriginal myths all across Australia.

AUSTRALIA

Did you know?

• The white settlers of Australia thought that the bunyip was more like a shaggy, harmless grazing animal with a doglike face. It is possible that tales of the bunyip were inspired by an extinct mammal, the diprotodon, which was the size of a rhinoceros.

• Some people suggest that the bunyip is just a seal that has swum up rivers from the sea. Others say that the cry of the bunyip is actually the booming sound of the shy Australasian bittern bird.

• In Australia, there is a river named the Bunyip River and also a town named Bunyip in the state of Victoria.

• In 1851, after a bunyip washed up on the banks of Fiery Creek, Victoria, an outline image of a bunyip was carved by Aborigines into the riverbank.

Langsuir

HAIR
The langsuir has beautiful long black hair, but unlike other female vampires, she is not dangerous to men. She only wants babies (or fish).

NECK
The feeding hole at the back of the langsuir's neck should be filled with her own hair. That way, she can be tamed.

HANDS
The langsuir has particularly long nails, which she uses to grab hold of the fish or babies she plans to eat. If her nails are cut, she can be brought under control.

SKIN
The langsuir's skin is very pale. She cannot go out during the day because she is allergic to sunlight. She hides in the forest or under rocks in the river until nightfall.

According to Malaysian mythology, if a woman dies in childbirth or shortly afterward, she will turn into a type of banshee known as langsuir. To prevent this, glass beads should be put in her mouth, hen's eggs tucked under each armpit, and needles placed in the palms of her hands. This way the langsuir cannot make her terrifying shriek, she cannot wave her arms and use them as wings, or use her nails.

If, however, she does become a langsuir, she will suck the blood of infants. If a langsuir is caught, she can be tamed by cutting her nails short and stuffing her long hair into the feeding hole in the back of her neck.

ACTUAL SIZE

▶ THE YOUNG MOTHER WAS CARRYING HER NEWBORN BABY in a sling through the woods when the langsuir appeared. She was terrified as the langsuir reached to take the baby, but she twisted the langsuir's long hair and stuffed it into the feeding hole in her neck. The mother then cut off the langsuir's long nails, which made her tame. The next day, the langsuir met a man in town and they married. They were happy and had a daughter, but at a village dance her langsuir spirit took her over again and she flew off into the forest forever.

Where in the world?

The langsuir comes from Malaysia in southeastern Asia. She may also change at night into a night owl with unusually long claws.

●MALAYSIA

Did you know?

• Sometimes, even placing only a single hair in the langsuir's feeding hole is all that is necessary to tame her.

• A similar vampire-like ghost from Malaysian folklore is the pontianak, which is the ghost of a child who died while being born. Unlike the langsuir, the pontianak is beautiful and attacks men. A pontianak can be tamed by sticking a nail into the hole in its neck. The city of Pontianak on the island of Borneo is named after this mythical creature.

• The word langsuir comes from the Malay word "helang," meaning eagle. Langsuirs are also believed to be able to fly.

• Langsuirs are most likely found near rivers and the sea. If they cannot find human flesh, they will eat fish.

Zahhak

HORNS
Zahhak has devil's horns.
He is cunning, strong, and
possessed of all possible
sins. He rules with the help
of demons called daevas.

SERPENTS
Two brave cooks in
Zahhak's kitchen saved the
lives of many men by
serving sheep's brains
instead of human brains to
Zahhak's serpent-heads.

WINGS
Zahhak is an "azi," which
means "serpent" or "dragon."
With his dragon wings he
flew over enemies, defeating
the soldiers and terrifying
the people.

BODY
In some versions, Zahhak appears as
a man with snakes growing out of his
cheeks. But in earlier versions,
Zahhak is a three-headed dragon.

Zahhak was the son of the ruler, but as a young man he was easily influenced by evil advisers. One persuaded Zahhak to kill his father by digging a pit and covering it with leaves. His father fell in and died, making Zahhak ruler. His adviser kissed Zahhak on both cheeks and immediately two snake heads grew out of his face.

ACTUAL SIZE

These needed to be fed with two human brains every day. With the help of demons, Zahhak ruled as a tyrant for a thousand years. It is believed that, at the end of the world, he will return and kill one in three humans and animals, before he is destroyed.

▶ ZAHHAK HAD VISIONS THAT HE WAS GOING TO BE ATTACKED. He ordered his men to find and kill this attacker, but learned that it was only a nine-year-old boy, Fredon, and that Fredon had already fled. Later, Fredon led an army against Zahhak's palace. Fredon attacked Zahhak and snakes and scorpions burst from the wounds. But the god Ormazd told Fredon not to kill Zahhak, because then the world would become overrun with these creatures. Instead, Fredon imprisoned Zahhak in a cave beneath Mount Damavand, where he remains until the end of time.

Where in the world?

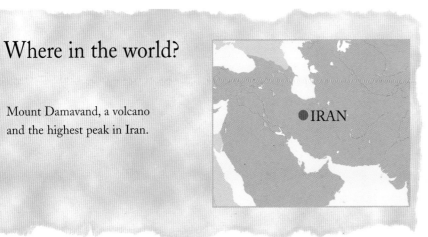

Mount Damavand, a volcano and the highest peak in Iran.

IRAN

Did you know?

• Tales of Zahhak, who is also known as Azhi Dahaka and Dahag, exist in Persian and Arabic folklore. The original story appears in Zoroastrian religious texts.

• A blacksmith called Kava had 18 children, but Zahhak had served 17 of them to the snakes in his cheeks. Zahhak showed mercy on the eighteenth child, who was in prison, but this still didn't make Kava a supporter of Zahhak.

• With his brother Spitiyura, Zahhak attacked Yima (Jamshid), a hero who had grown arrogant. They cut him in half with a saw.

• Fredon attacked Zahhak with a mace specially made from the head of an ox. In Zahhak's dream he saw three warriors attacking him, one with a mace, and then saw himself dragged off to a mountain. The other two attackers might have been Yima's daughters, Arnavaz and Shahrnavaz, whom Fredon had liberated from Zahhak's prison.

The Giant from Sinbad's Third Voyage

NOSE
When he was asleep, the giant's snoring sounded like a lamb dying in agony.

STICK
The giant used the stick to skewer one of Sinbad's sailors each night and cook him over the fire like a kabob.

HANDS
Sinbad said that the giant's nails were like a lion's claw. The giant picked up each sailor and examined him, turning him over in his palm, like a butcher choosing the best cut of meat.

FEET
When the giant had chosen which soldier to eat, he threw the sailor on the ground and stamped on him, killing him before skewering him to be cooked over a fire.

SIZE
The giant was as tall as a large date tree.

The giant had "eyes like coals of fire, teeth like a boar's tusks, and a big gape like the mouth of a well." Also, his lips were like a camel's but reached down to his chest, his ears fell over his shoulder blades, and his nails were like a lion's claws. Sinbad's ship had gone off course and now he and his fellow sailors were marooned on a desert island. Each night, the giant came to eat another member of their crew. During the day the giant left them in peace, but how were they going to escape from the island?

ACTUAL SIZE

▶ AT NIGHT THE GIANT PICKED THE FATTEST SAILOR, skewered him on a spit, and cooked him over a fire like a kabob. Sinbad's sailors were terrified and thought they would rather jump in the sea than be eaten, but Sinbad had a plan. The men built a raft and on the third night after the giant had fallen asleep, the sailors took two large sticks and drove them into the giant's eyes. Now blind, the giant raged after Sinbad and the sailors as they escaped to their raft.

Where in the world?

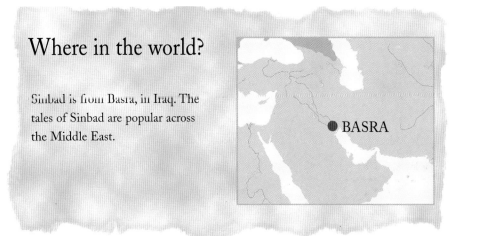

Sinbad is from Basra, in Iraq. The tales of Sinbad are popular across the Middle East.

● BASRA

Did you know?

● After Sinbad escaped from the giant, he and two sailors found themselves on another island. A giant snake ate the other sailors, but Sinbad built a box the snake couldn't break into and hid in it.

● Sinbad's adventures appear in the story "Sinbad the Sailor and Sinbad the Porter," where a poor porter called Sinbad is invited into the palace of a merchant, also called Sinbad, who tells the porter his tales.

● The tales of Sinbad are often included in the collection of stories known as *A Thousand and One Nights*, which dates from the tenth century. However, Sinbad was added to the collection only in the nineteenth century.

● Sinbad's escape from the giant is similar to the Greek myth of Odysseus and the one-eyed giant Polyphemus. In that story, Odysseus is caught on Polyphemus's island until he blinds the giant and escapes.

The Sorcerer from Aladdin

HEADSCARF
The sorcerer came from northwestern Africa, a long way from Aladdin's home in the story in Central Asia.

RING
This is the ring the sorcerer gave to Aladdin. The sorcerer didn't realize that the ring, when rubbed, would release the genie of the ring, who would help Aladdin.

KNIFE
The sorcerer carried a knife, but he never had to use it. Instead, he used his cunning, lying to Aladdin and getting Aladdin's wife to swap the old, magic lamp for a new, normal lamp.

CLOTHES
The sorcerer was already a wealthy man, but he wanted to use Aladdin to become hugely powerful, and he didn't care if Aladdin died in the process.

Aladdin is a poor, good-for-nothing boy whose father is dead. The sorcerer appears and says that he is Aladdin's father's brother. At first he is very kind to Aladdin. Then the sorcerer gives Aladdin a magic ring and sends him into a cave to bring back a special lamp. On returning, the sorcerer tries to snatch the lamp before Aladdin is safely out of the cave. Aladdin holds onto the lamp and the sorcerer traps him inside the cave. Alone, Aladdin cries and rubs the ring. A genie appears, granting Aladdin's wish to be free. But Aladdin hasn't seen the last of the sorcerer yet.

ACTUAL SIZE

▶ WITH THE HELP OF THE GENIE OF THE LAMP, Aladdin grows rich and marries the most beautiful woman of the city, Badr-al-Budr. But while Aladdin is away, the sorcerer reappears and tricks Badr-al-Budr into giving him the magic lamp. He takes Badr-al-Budr and her palace with him to Africa. The genie of the ring helps Aladdin get to Africa, where, disguised as a beggar, he enters the palace. He gives Bad-al-Budr a drug that she puts in the sorcerer's wine, killing him. Then Aladdin and Badr-al-Budr return home with their palace.

Where in the world?

The story of Aladdin is set in China but it comes from the Middle East and was written down in Aleppo, in Syria.

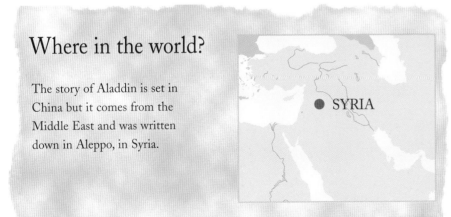

● SYRIA

Did you know?

● After Aladdin has killed the sorcerer, the sorcerer's brother appears. Disguised as a wise woman, he also tries to trick Aladdin, but Aladdin kills him with a dagger.

● In the final part of the story, the sorcerer (in disguise) suggests that the palace display the egg of the roc, a mythical giant bird of prey. This is the only wish the genie cannot grant Aladdin because the genie's master was a roc bird.

● Like Sinbad, the tale of Aladdin often appears in editions of the tenth-century story collection *A Thousand and One Nights*, but it was added to these stories only in the eighteenth century.

● Although the story is of Middle Eastern origin, the oldest surviving written version of the story is not in Arabic, but was written in French in 1709.

The Wolf from The Three Little Pigs

LEGS
The wolf is clever enough to climb onto the roof of the third little pig's house, but not clever enough to think what hot pots might be at the bottom of a chimney.

TEETH
The wolf's sharp teeth quickly finish off the first two little pigs. But the third little pig is too clever for him.

LUNGS
The wolf's breath is so powerful, and the first two little pigs' houses so fragile, that he can huff and puff and blow their houses down.

MOUTH
The wolf's mouth drips with the blood of the first two little pigs he has already eaten.

The wolf uses his strength and intelligence to try to capture the pigs to eat them. The first little pig builds his house out of straw and the wolf blows it down and eats the pig. The second pig builds his house out of wood, but the wolf blows it down and eats him, too. The third little pig builds his house out of brick. The wolf can't blow it down. He climbs onto the roof and goes down the chimney, but the pig puts a pot of water on the fire. The wolf lands in the hot water and is cooked and eaten by the pig.

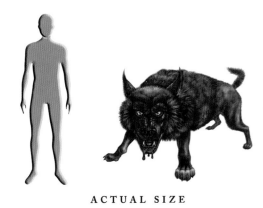

ACTUAL SIZE

▶ "I'LL HUFF AND I'LL PUFF AND I'LL BLOW YOUR HOUSE DOWN!" cries the wolf and he devours the first two little pigs. The third little pig is in a brick house, so the wolf tries to tempt him out by telling him about the turnips in the field, about the apples in the orchard, and finally about the local fair. But each time the little pig gets up before the wolf, takes the turnips, the apples, and butter from the fair, and is home before the wolf can catch him.

Where in the world?

The story of "The Three Little Pigs" first appeared in a book in a collection of English folk tales, but the story is known worldwide.

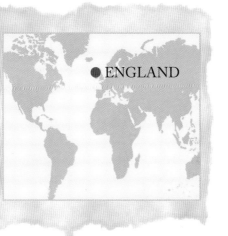

●ENGLAND

Did you know?

● "Little pig! Little pig! Let me come in!" cries the wolf each time he knocks on the door of one of the pig's houses. "No! Not by the hair of my chinny chin chin!" answer the little pigs.

● The three little pigs and the wolf appear in all the *Shrek* movies. In the second movie, they help look after Shrek and Fiona's home when the two of them are away visiting the kingdom of Far Far Away.

● In some of the versions of the story, the first two little pigs aren't eaten but manage to escape to the third little pig's house.

● There are similar versions of the story where the pigs are replaced by Br'er Rabbit and the wolf is replaced by a fox.

The Giant from Jack and the Beanstalk

HANDS
The giant's hands are as wide as a door.

CLUB
The giant comes after Jack with the club that he uses for killing humans and also calves (he eats three for breakfast). Swinging his club, he chases Jack down the beanstalk.

NOSE
He may not look very smart, but the giant has an excellent sense of smell when it comes to detecting the presence of humans.

TEETH
"Fe, Fi, Fo, Fum! I smell the blood of an Englishman. Be he alive, or be he dead, I'll grind his bones to make my bread," roars the giant. He has lost many teeth crunching on human bones.

The giant lives with his giant wife in a huge house high up in the clouds. On his belt hang three cows' calves that he has killed that morning. He's planning on eating a couple of them for breakfast, but then he smells Jack's human blood. The giant calls out: "Fe, Fi, Fo, Fum! I smell the blood of an Englishman. Be he alive, or be he dead, I'll grind his bones to make my bread." The giant's wife has hidden Jack in the oven and the giant doesn't find him. Then, when the giant is asleep, Jack steals some of the giant's gold coins and climbs back down the beanstalk.

ACTUAL SIZE

▶ THE THIRD AND LAST TIME JACK CLIMBS UP THE BEANSTALK, he hides in a big copper pot. The giant and his wife realize that Jack has been stealing from them and they look in the oven where Jack had hidden before. Jack climbs out of the copper pot and steals a talking harp from the giant. The harp calls out to the giant and the giant chases Jack down the beanstalk. When Jack is at the bottom of the beanstalk, he cuts it down, killing the giant. With their riches, Jack and his mother live happily ever after.

Where in the world?

The story "Jack and the Beanstalk" originates in England. It was first written down in the 1700s.

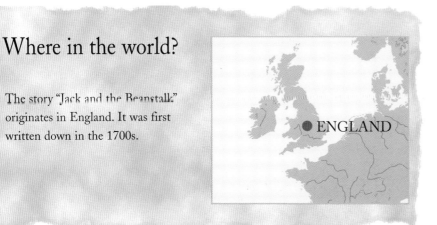

● ENGLAND

Did you know?

• The second time Jack climbs up the beanstalk, he steals from the giant a hen that lays golden eggs.

• In William Shakespeare's play *King Lear* (written between 1603 and 1606), the character Edgar, pretending to be insane, says: "Fie, foh, and fum, I smell the blood of a British man."

• When Jack's mother sends him to market to sell their cow, Milky-White, he exchanges the cow for five magic beans. His mother is very angry, but the beans grow into the beanstalk.

• There is a similar British story called "Jack the Giant Killer" set during the time of the legendary King Arthur. In this story, Jack is a strong and clever boy who kills several giants, one of them because it kills cattle, another because it imprisons Jack.

Lambton Worm

JAWS
Not only did the Lambton Worm devour 20 gallons of milk a day, but its jaws were big enough to snap up any small children easily.

HEAD
The Lambton Worm had nine holes on either side of its head, but no one knows what these were for.

TAIL
Cutting off a piece of the Lambton Worm's tail couldn't kill it. The Lambton Worm would just reattach the piece and the wound would heal over. It seemed invincible.

BODY
The Lambton Worm started off as a small eel that was caught by a boy who was out fishing one day. But it grew big enough to wrap itself several times around whole hills.

In northeastern England, the Lambton Worm was known as a giant eel with nine holes on either side of its salamander-like head. It ate sheep, stopped cows from producing milk, and snatched away small children. When it had grown so large that it was too big for the river or a well, it climbed out and wrapped itself many times around hills and then Lambton Castle. There, it continued to terrorize the neighborhood,

ACTUAL SIZE

demanding 20 gallons of milk a day. Then, whenever knights or villagers tried to kill it by cutting a piece off of it, the worm simply killed the attackers and reattached the missing part of the body.

▶ JOHN LAMBTON, who as a boy had first fished the worm out of the river, was preparing to kill the worm. A witch gave him two pieces of advice. First, he should sew the heads of spears into his armor and, second, after killing the worm he must kill the first living thing he sees, or his family will be cursed. John found the worm in the river. His spears cut off pieces of the worm and these were washed away before the worm could heal itself. John killed the worm, but in their joy his family forgot about John having to kill the first thing he saw, and so they suffered the curse.

Where in the world?

The Lambton Worm is named after the family it terrorized on the Lambton Estate, County Durham, northeastern England. It was said to have been first found in the Wear River.

DURHAM

Did you know?

....

• John Lambton first caught the worm one Sunday when he was supposed to be in church. He caught it in a river but dropped it into a well. Years later, he went to fight as a knight in the crusades in the Holy Land to show his faith.

• Legend says that the marks of the worm can still be seen on Worm Hill in Fatfield and also Penshaw Hill, County Durham, England.

• The Lambton curse says that nine generations of Lambton lords will not die in their beds. This came true for four of the nine.

• Bram Stoker, author of the novel *Dracula*, also wrote a novel called *The Lair of the White Worm*, based on the Lambton Worm legend.

The Tanuki from Kachi-Kachi Yama

EYES
The tanuki tried to look as innocent and harmless as possible while he was tied up, to fool the farmer's wife into letting him go. Then, he could kill her.

ARMS
The tanuki said he had strong arms and that if the farmer's wife let him go, he could pound the barley for her. Instead, once he was let go, he hit her on the head and chopped her up.

VOICE
After the tanuki had killed the farmer's wife, he let out a blood-chilling "Meeeeeooowww!" And when the farmer accidentally ate his wife, the tanuki just laughed.

CLAWS
The tanuki would use his claws to dig up all the farmer's vegetables. Because of this, the farmer vowed to catch the tanuki and turn him into a tasty soup.

In Japanese folklore, the tanuki is known for being as jolly and mischievous but not bad. But in the folk tale "Kachi-Kachi Yama," the tanuki's tricks turn nasty. The troublesome tanuki was caught in a field by a farmer. Later, the farmer went to town and the tanuki begged the farmer's wife to free him. Once freed, the tanuki killed the farmer's wife and turned himself into her. Then, he made a soup using the flesh of the farmer's wife and served it to the farmer. Once the farmer had finished, the tanuki revealed himself, telling the farmer what he'd just eaten. Then, the tanuki fled.

ACTUAL SIZE

▶ LATER, A RABBIT TOLD THE FARMER that he would avenge the farmer's wife's death. The rabbit tricked and tortured the tanuki many times, one time dropping a bee's nest on top of the tanuki, then treating his wounds with pepper, and setting fire to wood the tanuki was carrying on his back. Then, the two had a contest to see who could build a boat and cross a lake the fastest. The rabbit made his boat out of wood, but the foolish tanuki made his out of mud. In the water the tanuki's boat dissolved.

Where in the world?

The tanuki are popular all over Japan. The folklore is thought to come from the Kamakura Period, between the twelfth and fourteenth centuries.

JAPAN

Did you know?

• At Shikoku Tanuki train station in Japan appears the slogan, "Our trains aren't made of mud," in reference to the "Kachi-Kachi Yama" tale.

• The title of the story comes from the part where the rabbit lights the wood the tanuki is carrying. In Japanese, "kachi-kachi" is the crackling sound burning wood makes. "Yama" means mountain. The rabbit says that it's a "fire-crackle mountain" making the burning sound, not the very wood that's beginning to burn the tanuki's back.

• There are statues of tanuki outside temples and restaurants all over Japan. But these tanuki, with their enormous bellies, are the trickster kind—who might cheat a merchant by using leaves for money—not mean tanukis.

• Tanuki are also real animals in Japan. Tanuki is the name for the Japanese raccoon dog.

Little Otik

HEAD
Little Otik kept the small branches on his stump and they looked a little like frizzy hair.

EYES
The man who found Little Otik cut two eye holes in his stump to make Little Otik look more like a baby.

MOUTH
At first, Little Otik had only a little slit cut by the man for a mouth. But Little Otik grew so quickly that very soon his mouth was as big as his body had first been just hours earlier.

ARMS
Little Otik's branches were smoothed down to become two arms and his twigs became ten fingers.

ROOTS
The man smoothed Little Otik's tree roots to make them into ten toes.

A very poor man and his wife desperately wanted to have a baby but were unable to. One day in the forest, the man dug out a tree stump that was shaped just like a little baby. When he showed his wife, she was delighted. She wrapped the wooden baby in a quilt and sang to it. Then, the baby woke up and cried: "I'm so hungry, mother." The woman fed the baby everything she could find, but he was still hungry and growing as big as a barrel. Then, it ate her, her husband, and some pigs and sheep. And still it was growing.

ACTUAL SIZE

▶ AS THE WOODEN BABY DEVOURED A FIELD OF CABBAGES, an old woman farmer shouted at it to stop. It told her everything it had eaten so far and that it would now eat her. But just as it reached to gobble her up, she flicked her hoe at its massive stomach. The wooden baby fell down dead and out of the stomach came pigs and a farmer, sheep and a shepherd, a horse and cart, and finally the poor man and his wife. The poor couple were very happy for the rest of their lives not to have a baby.

Where in the world?

The story of the wooden baby, also known as Little Otik (Otesanek), comes from Bohemia in the Czech Republic.

CZECH
REPUBLIC

Did you know?

● The tale of the wooden baby was first published by Czech author K.J. Erben in the nineteenth century in his collection *Tales from Bohemia*, but the story itself comes from older folklore.

● The wooden baby is similar to the story from the movie and musical *Little Shop of Horrors*, in which a plant grows to have an appetite that is never satisfied, and so it eats people.

● The wooden baby also ate a milkmaid and her wheelbarrow full of clover and the shepherd's sheepdog, and still it was hungry.

● In 2001, the story of Little Otik was also made into a Czech animated and live action film called *Greedy Guts* (*Otesanek*) about a present-day couple and a wooden baby.

The Ogre from The Flea

SIZE
There are giants and there are big giants and then there was the ogre, which was the biggest giant you could ever imagine.

FACE
The ogre had such an ugly face that when he passed by, even tough soldiers would have to look away, pigs and cows would look up from their eating and stare, and flowers would wilt.

SKULL
In his hand, he carried a human skull that he used as a teapot. The nose was like a spout.

BELT
From his belt hung the legs and arms of people he had killed and would later eat. He offered them to his wife the princess, but she would eat only pea soup.

A king raised a flea until it was as big as a sheep. Then, he had it skinned and offered his beautiful daughter Porziella's hand in marriage to any man who could guess what animal the skin came from. No one knew the right answer until the ugliest, most scary ogre in all the land guessed the correct answer. The king had to allow the ogre to marry Porziella and the ogre took her to his palace, which was decorated with the bones of the people he had eaten. Crying at her window, Porziella told her story to an old woman whose seven sons were giants and they rescued the princess.

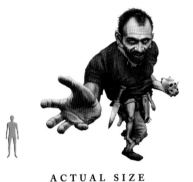

ACTUAL SIZE

▶ THE OGRE WENT SEARCHING FOR HIS MISSING WIFE, but the seven sons blocked his path: one listened for the ogre's footsteps; another washed his hands, making a sea of soapsuds; another turned a piece of iron into a field of razors; one turned a stick into a whole forest; another turned water into a river; and another turned a stone into a tower. The sons and Porziella hid inside the tower, but the ogre began climbing up. The youngest son cut the ogre's head off. The sons were rewarded and Porziella married a prince.

Where in the world?

"The Flea" is set in fairy-tale land, but the writer collected stories from all over Italy and wrote them down in the dialect of Naples.

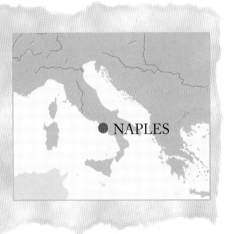

● NAPLES

Did you know?

• "The Flea" is an Italian story that was collected by Giambattista Basile and published in 1634, two years after he died. Basile's book of fifty fairy tales, *The Tale of Tales* (*Il Pentamerone*), also includes the earliest-known written versions of "Cinderella," "Snow White," and "Rapunzel."

• The king first catches the flea because it bites him. But seeing how handsome the insect is, he can't bear to kill it. So, he puts it in a jar and feeds it.

• Before the ogre touches and smells the flea-sheep skin and correctly identifies it, others guess that it's the skin of a giant cat, a crocodile, or an ape.

• When the ogre presents Porziella with human bodies for dinner he says: "Now, wife, you cannot complain that I don't take good care of you. You'll never be short of food with me."

Lord Voldemort

BRAIN
Voldemort can read people's minds, but they have no idea that it has happened. Unlike other wizards, he can also fly unsupported—he doesn't need a broomstick.

HEAD
Voldemort's head is like a skull and is hairless, but it wasn't always like that. Before he became corrupted, he was a handsome and charming man with black hair.

FACIAL FEATURES
Lord Voldemort's nose is almost nonexistent, he doesn't have any lips, and his skin is very pale. Voldemort's eyes are red with tiny, catlike slits for pupils.

BODY
Lord Voldemort's body is almost as thin as a skeleton. But this is not a sign of weakness. He is the most powerful wizard in the world.

Lord Voldemort is so feared in the world of Hogwarts School that barely any witch or wizard dares mention his name. Instead, the Harry Potter characters call him "He-Who-Must-Not-Be-Named" or the "Dark Lord." An evil wizard, Voldemort is the archenemy of Harry Potter, who, according to a prophecy, has the power to defeat the "Dark Lord." When he tried to kill Harry as a baby, Voldemort's body was magically destroyed. His spirit survived, though, and now only Harry's blood can restore his body. Voldemort wants to become immortal, he enjoys hurting others, and he doesn't understand friendship or love. His fear of death is his weakness.

ACTUAL SIZE

▶ THROUGH TRICKERY, HARRY POTTER found himself transported to Little Hangleton, the village of Voldemort's ancestors. There, into a cauldron in the graveyard, a bundle was dropped, along with a hand, a bone from Voldemort's father, and some of Harry's blood. From the mixture, Voldemort appeared, his body restored. He summoned his Death Eaters and challenged Harry to a duel. But once Voldemort's and Harry's wands touched, they became magically locked. Ghostly faces appeared of people Voldemort had killed, including Harry's parents. Rather than killing Harry, Voldemort became distracted and Harry, seizing his chance, escaped.

Where in the world?

Hogwarts School, somewhere in Scotland. Unfortunately, Muggles—nonmagical people— can't see it. To them, the school just looks like ruins.

●SCOTLAND

Did you know?

• Voldemort appears in all the Harry Potter novels except the third book, *Harry Potter and the Prisoner of Azkaban* and the sixth book, *Harry Potter and the Half-Blood Prince*.

• Harry Potter author J.K. Rowling has said that if Voldemort looked into the Mirror of Erised (the mirror that shows you your desire—Erised being *desire* spelled backward), he would see "himself—all powerful and eternal." If he saw his boggart—what he feared most—it would be his own dead body.

• Voldemort can talk to serpents. His wand is made of yew, the sap of which is poisonous. Harry's wand is made of holly.

• Voldemort wants to eliminate all Muggles (nonmagical people) from the wizarding world. Then, he believes, he can conquer both the wizarding and the Muggle world.

Gollum

VOICE
Gollum hisses and whines at the hobbits. He mutters to himself about his obsession with the One Ring.

BODY
Gollum's body has grown pale and thin with age. Once, he was a normal man, but the One Ring corrupted him. Under the spell of the One Ring, Gollum lived for hundreds of years (he is between 570 and 600 years old at the end of the story).

TEETH
Gollum has only six teeth, which he sharpens into points using a rock.

POCKETS
In his pockets, Gollum keeps a tooth-sharpening rock, goblin teeth, wet shells, and a scrap of bat wing.

MUSCLES
Though very skinny, Gollum is actually much stronger than he appears. Also, his obsession with the Ring is a force, which strengthens him.

From J. R. R. Tolkien's novels *The Hobbit* and *The Lord of the Rings*, Gollum was once a hobbit called Sméagol, but when he found the Ring, it possessed and corrupted him. He both loved and hated the Ring, just as he loved and hated himself. Gollum was nasty, bitter, and sly, but could also be playful, grateful, and helpful. When he lost the Ring, he spent the rest of his life trying to find it. And when he learned that Frodo Baggins had the Ring, the test for Gollum was whether he could resist the temptation to possess the Ring, or let Frodo destroy it.

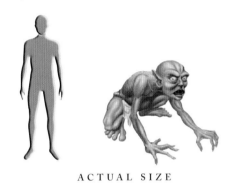

ACTUAL SIZE

▶ SMÉAGOL AND HIS COUSIN DÉAGOL WENT FISHING. A big fish pulled Déagol into the water, but there he found the Ring. He showed it to Sméagol, who immediately fell under the Ring's spell and demanded it as a birthday present. The two began fighting and Sméagol fought so viciously that he strangled Déagol. Sméagol used the Ring's power of invisibility for stealing, spying, and upsetting his friends and relatives. Eventually, his family rejected him. He retreated to a cavern in the Misty Mountains and the Ring's sinister influence twisted his body and his mind.

Where in the world?

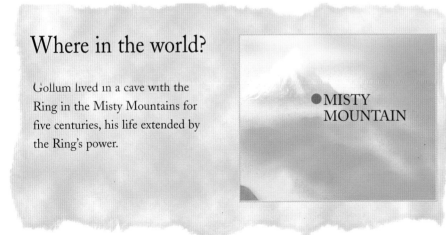

Gollum lived in a cave with the Ring in the Misty Mountains for five centuries, his life extended by the Ring's power.

●MISTY MOUNTAIN

Did you know?

• Gollum spoke in his own special way, adding "es" to words to make "two birdses" or "two hobbitses." He often referred to himself as "Sméagol" not "I." And the Ring was his "precious."

• Sméagol became known as Gollum because of the horrible swallowing sound he made.

• In his search for the Ring, Gollum became a spy for Shelob, a monstrous spider, whom he worshipped. He would bring her food and planned to feed Frodo to her.

• Gollum first appeared in *The Hobbit*, living on an island on a lake near a network of caves. He ate fish and small goblins, but he had lost the Ring in the caves. Then, the hobbit Bilbo Baggins stumbled into the caves, found the Ring, and kept it.

Red Weed

DEADLY
Although deadly, after the Martians were defeated, the red weed turned to ash and was blown away by the wind.

VEGETABLE
Although it was not an animal that directly killed people, the red weed could choke other plants and grow over buildings, trapping people inside.

BLOOD RED
In the 2005 movie *War of the Worlds*, the aliens used human blood to fertilize the red weed, adding to its red color.

ROOTS
The red weed spread swiftly over the English countryside. It grew particularly well near water sources and could very quickly clog up rivers and streams.

CREEPER
The red weed is sometimes also called "red swamp" or "red creeper."

When the Martians invade Earth in H. G. Wells's novel *The War of the Worlds*, they bring red weeds with them. While the Martians cannot live in the Earth's atmosphere without the protection of their huge tripod machines, the red weed thrives and spread rapidly across the English landscape. Near a source of water, it grows even more quickly and soon clogs up rivers and streams. It is the red weed that, in the story, supposedly grows on Mars and gives the planet its dull red color. Before the end of the story, the red weed has choked the entire native plant life on Earth.

ACTUAL SIZE

▶ WHEN HE WOKE UP, HE LOOKED OUT FROM THE WINDOW high up on the cellar way. Outside, he could see where his pond had been, but now it was covered from side to side by red weed. Where the fountain had been in the middle of the pond was a mound of red weed. The water mill was completely clogged—it was a wheel of red weed. The cellar shook. A Martian's tripod must have been lurching above the house. Then, a tentacle burst through the glass and dragged the man out of the window.

Where in the world?

H.G. Wells's novel *The War of the Worlds* (1898) is set in London and in the town of Woking, southwest of London.

LONDON ●

Did you know?

• The red weed has a metallic taste. At night it glows purple.

• The red weed is perhaps inspired by species of plants that are new to a country and very difficult to control. In Britain in the nineteenth century, Japanese knotweed was introduced and then spread very rapidly. In the USA, kudzu, a vine from East Asia, grows over trees and eventually kills them.

• H. G. Wells's Martians have a "V-shaped mouth surrounded by Gorgon groups of tentacles." (The Gorgons were terrifying women of Greek mythology with live, hissing snakes for hair.) The Martians feed on human blood.

• The Martians have difficulty with Earth's atmosphere and so retreat to their cylinders. But there they assemble tripods (three-legged fighting machines), each of which has a heat ray and a chemical weapon known as "black smoke."

Saruman

HAND
As a wizard, Saruman could throw power and cast spells through his hand. He could slam doors, create fireworks, and throw people across rooms with just a wave of his hand.

VOICE
Saruman had a very persuasive voice. Tolkien wrote that it was "low and melodious, its very sound an enchantment . . . it was a delight to hear the voice speaking . . ."

STAFF
Saruman's staff was the only weapon he carried with him at all times. It was like a wizard's wand, and he could use his magic powers through it. Ultimately, Gandalf defeated Saruman and broke his staff.

ROBES
Saruman wore the white robes of a wizard throughout most of *The Lord of The Rings*. However, after he lost his power he returned to the Shire as a beggar.

One of the villains of J.R.R. Tolkien's novel *The Lord of the Rings,* Saruman the White is leader of the Istari—wizards, including Gandalf, who are sent to Middle-earth to challenge the Dark Lord Sauron. At first, Saruman is a force of good, but he becomes obsessed with the One Ring and corrupted by the idea of its power. He is building his own army of orcs and wolves to challenge

ACTUAL SIZE

Sauron and tries to persuade Gandalf to join him. He industrializes the green valley of Isengard, but in the end he is defeated by the simple technology of the hobbits and the treelike Ents.

► At SARUMAN'S FORTRESS IN ISENGARD, Gandalf sought Saruman's help in the fight against Sauron. But Saruman believed that it was too late to defeat Sauron and that they should become allies with the Dark Lord. Gandalf resisted this idea, but before he could leave the fortress, Saruman slammed the doors shut. The two great wizards fought with their staffs, throwing each other across the castle floors. But Saruman was the stronger and seized both staffs. Victorious, he imprisoned Gandalf in the tower of Orthanc, the black tower of Isengard.

Where in the world?

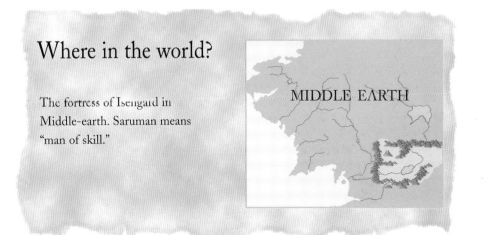

MIDDLE EARTH

The fortress of Isengard in Middle-earth. Saruman means "man of skill."

Did you know?

• The army Saruman is building includes Uruk-hai, an advanced breed of orcs that feed on human flesh. They are bigger, stronger, and faster than normal orcs, and have the ability to travel during daylight.

• The tower of Orthanc, where Gandalf is imprisoned by Saruman, is one of the towers in *The Two Towers,* the second volume of *The Lord of the Rings.* The other tower is Minas Morgul, a base for many of Sauron's orcs.

• In the end, Saruman is set free by Gandalf and is offered the chance to lead a good life, but he rejects it.

• When Saruman dies, his body immediately shrivels away to skin and bones, revealing "long years of death." Over the body rises "a pale shrouded figure."

Tharks

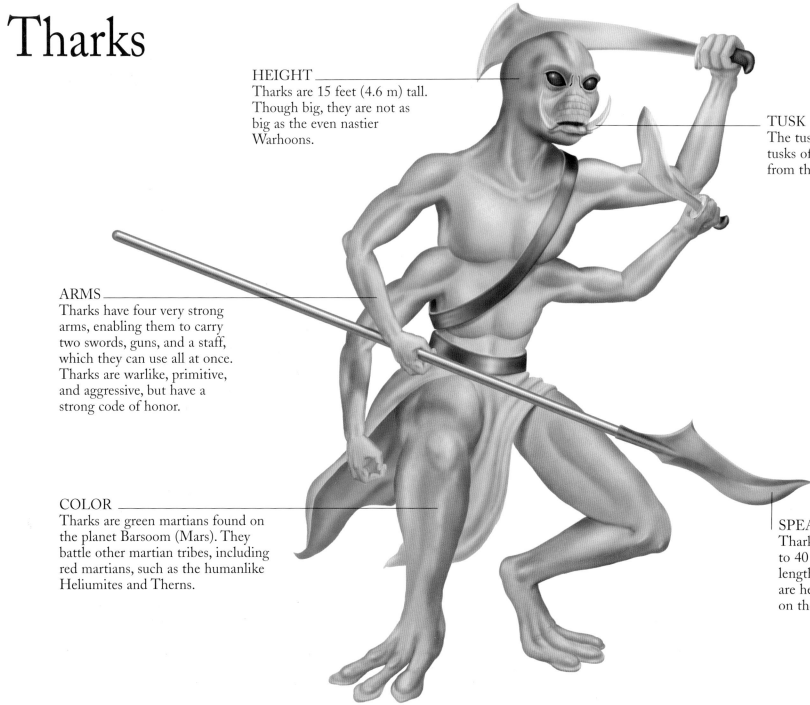

HEIGHT
Tharks are 15 feet (4.6 m) tall.
Though big, they are not as
big as the even nastier
Warhoons.

TUSK
The tusks of a Thark resemble the
tusks of a walrus, but they grow up
from their lower jaws, not down.

ARMS
Tharks have four very strong
arms, enabling them to carry
two swords, guns, and a staff,
which they can use all at once.
Tharks are warlike, primitive,
and aggressive, but have a
strong code of honor.

COLOR
Tharks are green martians found on
the planet Barsoom (Mars). They
battle other martian tribes, including
red martians, such as the humanlike
Heliumites and Therns.

SPEAR
Thark spears are up
to 40 ft (12.2 m) in
length. To use, they
are held in two arms
on the same side.

Tharks are a tribe of warriors from the planet Barsoom in the "John Carter of Mars" stories written by Edgar Rice Burroughs. Tharks are a cruel, warlike race that enjoy torture, but also have a strong sense of honor. They are enemies of the Warhoons, who are even more savage than the Tharks. The Tharks are first encountered when Confederate John Carter is mysteriously transported from Arizona to the planet Barsoom (Mars) at the end of the American Civil War. Carter finds that because of the different atmosphere of Barsoom, he is stronger than on Earth and he soon rises to become a leader of the Tharks.

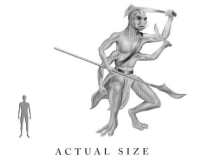

ACTUAL SIZE

▶ JOHN CARTER WAS HIDING FROM THE APACHE IN A CAVE IN ARIZONA. He was wounded and thought he was dying, then suddenly he found himself in another desert, but on a different planet. Giant, green, multiarmed men were running toward him, screaming a terrifying war cry. John Carter began to run and found that he could outrun them. In fact, he could run much faster than he could on Earth. Another group of green martians blocked his way, but Carter found that he was also stronger than they were, and he killed one.

Where in the world?

John Carter was in Arizona when he was transported to Barsoom, the planet Mars.

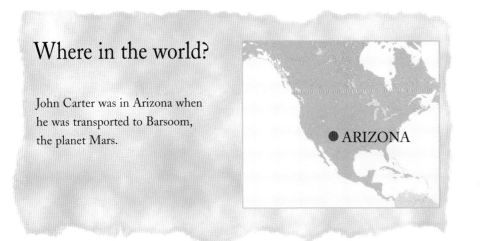

●ARIZONA

Did you know?

• In the same year that American Edgar Rice Burroughs first wrote the "John Carter of Mars" stories (1912), he also wrote the novel *Tarzan of the Apes*, a story about a boy in Africa who is raised by apes after the death of his parents.

• Tharks have no culture and cannot write. They do not form families and do not understand friendship.

• The first Mars book, *A Princess of Mars*, was published as *Under The Moon Of Mars* in 1912. For the publication, Edgar Rice Burroughs used the pen name Norman Bean.

• Tharks ride aggressive animals called thoats. Tharks fight with swords, lances, and a type of gun that uses the radioactive substance radium as ammunition. They are not intelligent enough to build their own weapons, but steal firearms from the red martians.

The Snow Queen

FACE
The Snow Queen had a beautiful face, but when she spoke her breath was freezing.

SNOWFLAKES
Around the Snow Queen fluttered snowflakes larger than you normally see. Even without a magnifying glass, you could see their unusual shapes: some were like snakes knotted together, some like small, fat bears with their hair standing on ends, and others looked like ugly porcupines.

COAT
When the Snow Queen stopped her sleigh, Kai was freezing and frightened. She wrapped him in her white fur coat and he had never felt so comfortable and warm. He forgot all about his old life in the city.

CLOTHES
The Snow Queen was tall and elegant and wore the finest white robes and a bearskin.

Just as worker bees have a queen, snowflakes have the Snow Queen. They guard her while she sits on a throne on top of a frozen lake at her palace situated north of Norway. She travels around the world with the winter snow. Be careful if you see a swirl of snowflakes—that is where she is most likely to be seen. When the boy Kai first sees the Snow Queen, she waves to him through a swirl of snow, asking him to follow her, but he is scared so he turns away from her. Later, she catches him and traps him in her ice palace.

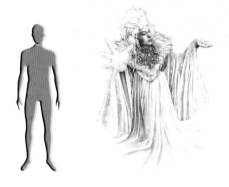

ACTUAL SIZE

▶ KAI WENT TO THE MARKET SQUARE and hitched his sled to a strange white sleigh. Immediately, the sleigh shot off and dragged Kai outside the city. When it stopped, the Snow Queen, a beautiful but intimidating woman, took Kai into the sleigh and wrapped him in her fur coat. She kissed him once to make him warm and a second time to make him forget his family and his friend, Gerda. But to kiss him a third time would have killed him. Then, they raced off to her ice palace in the far north.

Where in the world?

The Snow Queen's palace is on the island of Spitsbergen in the Arctic Circle off northern Norway. Even in summer, temperatures reach only 39 °F (4 °C).

SPITSBERGEN

Did you know?

• The Danish writer Hans Christian Andersen published the fairy tale "The Snow Queen" in 1845. Andersen wrote many fairy tales, including "The Ugly Duckling," "The Little Mermaid," and "The Emperor's New Clothes."

• The Snow Queen is similar to the White Witch in *The Chronicles of Narnia* written by C.S. Lewis. In both stories, the character wears a white fur coat and the White Witch turns Narnia into a snow-covered land.

• Kai's heart became frozen because he had caught a piece of glass from a broken magic mirror. The mirror only reflected and exaggerated the worst in people. Kai caught a piece in his eye and could no longer see the good in life. He stopped being friends with Gerda and was easily taken away by the Snow Queen.

Cthulhu

BRAIN
One of the scariest things about Cthulhu is that it knows so much more than humans do. The worries of humankind are insignificant next to the knowledge of the Cthulhu.

MOUTH
Green slime oozes out of Cthulhu's mouth.

FEET
The few eyewitnesses to Cthulhu who have survived described it as either walking or stumbling, but certainly slobbering and unstoppable: "After vigintillions [many millions] of years, great Cthulhu was loose again, and ravening for delight."

ARMS
Cthulhu's arms grab the sailors who find it on the island in the Pacific Ocean. Then, it either strangles them or eats them—or both.

The worshippers of this despicable beast would chant "In his house at R'lyeh, dead Cthulhu waits dreaming." They believed that Cthulhu was a god from an ancient religion who would rise again, and R'lyeh was the underwater city where Cthulhu was trapped. Around the world, crowds of people went crazy expecting its return. By the end of H. P. Lovecraft's short story "The Call of Cthulhu," it has

ACTUAL SIZE

risen again, and killed many people. Also, although it could be wounded, its wounds healed almost immediately. If humans had contact with it and it didn't kill them, the knowledge they learned from it drove them mad.

► SOME SAILORS FOUND AN ISLAND THAT WASN'T ON THE MAP. High on the rocks stood the nightmare ruin of a city. Among the crumbling buildings, the sailors managed to open an immense door and saw a terrible horror: Cthulhu squeezed its slimy way through the door, propelling itself toward them. It had waited a very long time. The sailors ran, but they couldn't all escape the power or speed of Cthulhu. The two sailors who made it to the ship were unable to speak for weeks, even after they had reached the mainland.

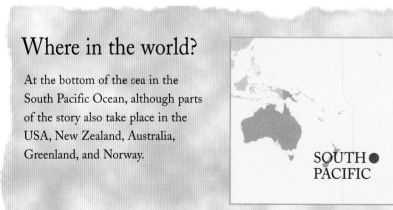

Where in the world?

At the bottom of the sea in the South Pacific Ocean, although parts of the story also take place in the USA, New Zealand, Australia, Greenland, and Norway.

SOUTH PACIFIC

Did you know?

• H. P. Lovecraft wrote the horror story "The Call of Cthulhu" in 1926. He wrote more stories with Cthulhu in them and other writers, such as Stephen King and Neil Gaiman, have written stories featuring Cthulhu.

• The phrase the worshippers of Cthulhu chant is: "Ph'nglui mglw'nafh Cthulhu R'lyeh wgah'nagl fhtagn." Can you say it? It means: "In his house at R'lyeh, dead Cthulhu waits dreaming."

• One of the scariest things about Cthulhu is that the people realize there is nothing they can do to save themselves. Cthulhu is older, wiser, and more powerful, and knows more than humans on Earth do about the universe.

• Although Cthulhu has been very influential in horror writing, Lovecraft thought his story was only average and it was rejected when he first submitted it to the magazine *Weird Tales*.

Loki

FACE
Loki had a very
handsome, pleasant
face, but his character
lurched very often
from sweet to nasty.

BRAIN
Loki enjoyed contests of
exchanging imaginative insults
with other gods. This was
known as flyting.

LIPS
Around Loki's lips are
the scars where
dwarves once sewed up
his mouth because he
talked too much.

BELT BUCKLE
Loki is a mysterious god and the
laughing face in a jester's hat on his
belt buckle reminds us of his trickster
side. He often helped the other gods
unravel a mess that he himself had
created in the first place.

SIZE
Loki was first a giant
before he became a god.

Loki is a god from Norse mythology. He is the father of the wolf Fenrir and the world serpent Jormungand. He is a shape-shifter, able to turn into a salmon, a seal, and a fly. At Ragnarök, the battle at the end of the world, Loki fights the god Heimdallr and they kill each other. Sometimes Loki assists other gods, at other times he's a trickster. However, for no reason, he is envious of the god Baldr. Loki arranges Baldr's death and then refuses to help bring Baldr back to life. For this, he is banished. He later escapes to fight at Ragnarök.

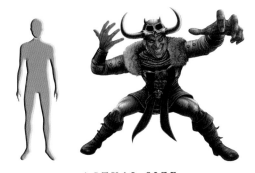

ACTUAL SIZE

▶ LOKI WOULDN'T WEEP WITH THE OTHER GODS FOR BALDR, and so they were unable to bring Baldr back from Hel (the underworld). For this reason, the gods tied Loki to a rock using the intestines of one of his sons. The goddess Skadi put a serpent above his head and the serpent dripped venom, which Loki's wife Sigyn collected to stop it from burning Loki. But when the bowl was full, she had to empty it and the venom that dripped onto Loki was so painful that it caused earthquakes.

Where in the world?

Across Scandinavia, but the Vikings took their beliefs with them beyond Scandinavia, and as a result a few monuments to Norse gods can be found in Britain.

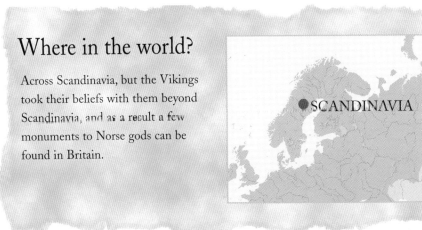

●SCANDINAVIA

Did you know?

• Loki, the god Thor, and two children sheltered in an immense building. They felt earthquakes all night, until they realized that they were sleeping in the glove of the giant Skrymir and that what they thought were earthquakes was Skrymir snoring.

• In one tale, Thor's hammer Mjöllnir was stolen. The thief Thrym would give it back only if the goddess Freyja married him. Freyja refused and Thor and Loki, dressed as women, went to Thrym's kingdom pretending to be Freyja and a friend. Just before the wedding ceremony, Thor saw Mjöllnir, hit Thrym with it, and escaped home with his hammer.

• When Loki infuriated the other gods by refusing to help Baldr, he hid himself by changing into a salmon.

• The myths predicted that Loki and Heimdallr would kill each other at Ragnarök, the battle at the end of the world.

Jormungand

MOUTH
Jormungand can spit venom powerful enough to kill a god, but this will happen only at the battle at the end of the world, when Jormungand and the god Thor fight. Thor kills Jormungand, but Jormungand's venom has also poisoned Thor.

TAIL
Jormungand was so big he could wrap himself around the world and bite his own tail. The movements of his body caused storms and tidal waves.

BODY
Jormungand was thrown into the sea by Odin, Loki's father, when he realized what a threat this powerful and poisonous serpent could be to the gods. However, in the sea Jormungand grew to gigantic proportions.

A giant sea serpent, Jormungand is one of the god Loki's three children, along with Hel, who is half a living woman, half a dead one, and Fenrir, a ferocious fox. The gods feel threatened by these children and throw Jormungand into the sea, where he grows so large that he can surround the Earth and grasp his own tail. It is said that when he lets go, the world will end. He fights the god Thor three times, the final battle predicted to happen at Ragnarök, where Jormungand will come out of the ocean and poison the sky. Thor will kill Jormungand, before dying himself from the serpent's venom.

ACTUAL SIZE

▶ THE SECOND TIME THOR AND JORMUNGAND MET, Thor went fighting with the giant Hymir. Thor cut the head off Hymir's largest ox to use as bait. Jormungand gripped the bait between his teeth. Then, Thor pulled so hard that his feet went through the bottom of the boat. The serpent came to the surface and looked into Thor's eyes. Jormungand dribbled poison and blood. Hymir was terrified. Thor reached for his hammer Mjöllnir to kill Jormungand, but Hymir cut the fishing line and Jormungand sank back into the depths of the waters.

Where in the world?

Scandinavia, but the fishing story is shown in Viking carvings in Scandinavia and Britain.

●SCANDINAVIA

Did you know?

● Jormungand's mother was a giantess. Jormungand's father Loki was a giant before he became a god.

● The first time Jormungand and Thor met, Jormungand was disguised as a giant cat and Thor had to lift him. He managed only to make the cat lift one leg, but it was enough to impress the giant king Utgarda-Loki.

● Jormungand (the Midgard Serpent) also appears in the Marvel Comics "Thor" series.

● In some versions of the boating story, Thor was so angry at losing Jormungand that he threw his hammer after the serpent and it killed Jormungand.

● Jormungand's other name is Midgardsorm, meaning the "worm of Midgard," the middle kingdom of people between the home of the gods and the underworld.

Theelgeth

NECK
Theelgeth didn't lose its head, it simply never had one. It was an "anaye," an alien god in Navajo mythology. But it did have a mouth where its neck would have been.

CLAWS
Theelgeth used its claws to attack the Navajo people so it could eat them.

HAIR
The Theelgeth was always described as being a hairy monster, a little like Yeti or Bigfoot.

BODY
With no eyes, ears, or nose, it has never been explained how the Theelgeth sensed where people were in order to eat them. Perhaps it had a different kind of sense. All we do know is that it was a man-eater.

M an-eating Theelgeth is one of the *anaye* (alien gods) of Navajo myth. Before the Navajo people reached the world we know, they passed through other worlds, among them, the Red World, the Blue World, and the Yellow World, escaping them, sometimes during a flood. If Navajo women had been sinful during their time in these worlds, they gave birth to anaye when they reached our world. Theelgeth was the first anaye born, and terrorized the Navajo people.

ACTUAL SIZE

When twin brothers Nayanezgani and Thobadzistshini returned from their dangerous journey to see their father Tshohanoai, they were armed with magic weapons, which they used to kill many of the anaye, including Theelgeth.

▶ NAYANEZGANI AND THOBADZISTSHINI now had magic arrows and armor with which to fight the anaye. They camped outside the settlement, near a lake where Theelgeth often came at night to drink. They waited until nighttime and then heard the earth-trembling footsteps of his approach. The brothers jumped out and attacked the beast, but Theelgeth easily knocked Nayanezgani through the air, leaving him unconscious. The beast bent over to eat him and Thobadzistshini fired his arrow into Theelgeth's back, through his body and out of his mouth. The beast fell down dead.

Where in the world?

The Navajo homeland is in the southwestern states around Colorado, Utah, New Mexico, and Arizona.

●SOUTHWESTERN USA

Did you know?

• Other anaye are Tshanahale, covered in feathers; Binyahe Ahani, twins with no arms or legs who could kill with a single glance; Yeitso, a fearsome giant whose hair grew into a rock so that he wouldn't fall over; and Delgeth, a flesh-eating antelope.

• Theelgeth is similar to the European and African blemyahs, which were headless but with eyes in their shoulders and mouths in their chests. However, the blemyahs didn't eat people.

• The only anaye that Nayanezgani and Thobadzistshini with the help of Tshohanoai failed to kill weren't monsters but Cold, Hunger, Old Age, and Poverty. According to legend, these were allowed to survive because they convinced the gods and goddesses that if they died, people would not appreciate the good things in life.

Set

SCEPTER
Set carried the "was scepter," a symbol of power. Was scepters were responsible for the well-being of the deceased and so were included in burial tombs.

BODY
Set looked part dog, part horse. Usually, Set was drawn as a man with a jackal or dog's head. When drawn as an animal, it was a combination of an aardvark, a donkey, and a jackal. Sometimes, Set was drawn as a Sha, a North African mythical dog with a straight forked tail.

ANKH SIGN
Like many Egyptians, Set carried the Ankh sign, which meant "eternal life."

Set was god of Upper Egypt and god of the Night. As lord of the desert, he was jealous of his brother Osiris, lord of vegetation. Set tricked his brother into climbing into a chest, which he sealed and threw in the Nile River. Isis, Osiris's wife, found the body, but Set cut it up into 14 pieces and scattered them. Isis collected the pieces and made a mummy out of Osiris's body. Osiris became king of the Underworld. His son Horus was hidden from Set to keep him safe and when he reached adulthood he continued the battle with Set.

ACTUAL SIZE

► SET AND HORUS HAD MANY CONTESTS TO SEE WHO SHOULD BE KING OF EGYPT. In one, Set scooped out Horus's eyes, but another god healed them. Later, Set suggested they build stone boats and have a race. Set made his boat out of mountain rock, but Horus made his out of wood painted to look like stone. Set's boat sank. In anger, he turned into a hippopotamus and shattered Horus's boat. Set was then killed by ten harpoons. Afterwards, Set's limbs were given to different gods, his bones to cats, and his fat to worms.

Where in the world?

Set was said to rule over Upper Egypt. His temple was at Nebet, near Luxor.

● EGYPT

Did you know?

● The horse, the antelope, the pig, the hippopotamus, and the crocodile were sacred to Set. In later myths, Set is shown as a donkey or with donkey's ears.

● His mother, Nut, was the sky goddess and his father, Geb, was the Earth god. Set was not born normally but burst violently out of the side of his mother's body.

● In later myths, Set became the god of chaos. Set and Horus also eventually became one god. In another version of the myth, Set didn't die but was banished and condemned forever to make thunder and frighten people.

● There is some historical basis to the story of Set and Horus: during the Second Dynasty (2890–2686 B.C.E.), there was a struggle between Upper Egypt and Lower Egypt.

Ammut

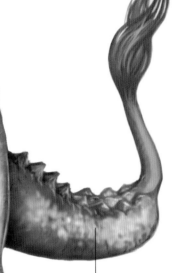

EYES
Ammut spent every day of her life watching the dead pass through the Underworld. Ammut looked at the fear in their eyes and saw their hope that they would reach immortality.

TAIL
Ammut was said to have the tail and mane of a lion and the body of a crocodile—two of the largest mammals known to the ancient Egyptians.

HEAD
Ammut had the head of a hippopotamus—a large, terrifying creature the Egyptians saw in the Nile River.

MOUTH
Ammut's mouth craved only one thing—human hearts. If the person was judged to have sinned too much in life, Ammut was given their heart to gobble down.

Ammut was a demon feared by ancient Egyptians. Her body was made up of a lion, a hippopotamus, and a crocodile because those were the three largest "man-eating" animals known to the ancient Egyptians. In the Underworld, a dead person's heart underwent judgment. If it was deemed impure, Ammut was given the heart to eat and the dead person was not allowed to continue his voyage to

ACTUAL SIZE

immortality. Once the heart was swallowed, the soul of the dead would become restless forever. Sometimes Ammut stood beside a lake of fire and watched as impure hearts were thrown into the lake to be destroyed.

▶ THE MAN KNEW HE HAD SINNED IN LIFE, but hoped his papyrus of spells was enough to persuade the gods in the Underworld to let him reach immortality. Entering the Underworld, he stopped at caves and gates, reading a spell to the animal-headed people. He passed each stage and finally reached the jackal-headed god Anubis, and Ammut. Anubis weighed the man's heart: was he sinful or not? The man had almost made it to immortality. But Anubis handed the heart to Ammut—the man had been too sinful in life and would not find peace in death.

Where in the world?

Ammut lived near the scales of justice in the Egyptian Underworld. Ancient Egyptian civilization developed along the Nile River.

● EGYPT

Did you know?

• In the Underworld, the test of a person's purity was the weight of their heart. If it weighed the same as the feather of Anubis, it was found to be pure. If it weighed more than the feather or less, then the heart was impure and was given to Ammut to eat or thrown into a lake.

• The Underworld was known as Duat, a vast area under the Earth, where not only the dead but some gods, such as Osiris, god of the underworld, lived. The sun god Ra traveled through Duat each night, starting from the west in order to arrive in the east in time for dawn each morning.

• Ammut was known as the "devourer of the dead."

• Ammut's image was thought to ward off evil. Though terrifying, she was a force for good, reminding people to live an honest life in order to die with a pure heart.

Humbaba

BREATH
Humbaba's foul breath could make the grass turn yellow, silence crickets, cause birds to lose their sense of direction, and kill people.

TAIL
Humbaba changed from a giant into a dragon when Gilgamesh and Enkidu arrived to kill him. His tail ended in a snake's head, which hissed and bit.

FIRE
Humbaba laughed and breathed fire at Gilgamesh, but the gods blew such strong winds back at Humbaba that he was trapped.

BODY
Humbaba was a giant with a lion's face and horny scales on his body. From his wild hair grew two bull's horns. He could hear sounds coming from more than 180 miles (290 km) away.

FEET
Humbaba had vulture's feet.

Humbaba was a giant who guarded the evergreen Cedar Forest. People were terrified of him because his shout was as powerful as a tidal wave, his whisper was like fire, his breath could kill, and his face was as ugly as intestines. It wasn't possible to sneak up on him because his hearing reached 180 miles (290 km) away. He didn't sleep and he was armed with seven terrors. The gods made him guardian of the forest and he threatened to devour anyone who entered. But Gilgamesh wanted to build a palace out of the best cedar wood and he wasn't going to be stopped by Humbaba.

ACTUAL SIZE

▶ WHEN GILGAMESH AND HIS FRIEND ENKIDU REACHED THE FOREST, Humbaba changed into a fire-breathing dragon and laughed that they looked as small as tortoises. Gilgamesh began to lose hope, but the gods took pity on him and blew 13 strong winds against Humbaba. The winds trapped Humbaba and darkened his face. He begged to be released, but Enkidu persuaded Gilgamesh to cut off the giant's head. They put it in a leather bag and floated it down the Euphrates River on a raft made of the wood they had chopped down.

Where in the world?

It is possible the cedar forests of the myth are actually found in the Zagros Mountains mainly in Iran or west of Mesopotamia in Lebanon.

●IRAN

Did you know?

● This story comes from the poem the Epic of Gilgamesh, the oldest parts of which date from the eighteenth century B.C.E. It is one of the most ancient stories in the world.

● Gilgamesh was a real person who ruled Uruk in Mesopotamia around 2600 B.C.E. The ruins of Uruk are located in Iraq.

● Enkidu was a wild man created by the gods as a rival to Gilgamesh who, as a ruler, was out of control. Enkidu and Gilgamesh fought at first, then became friends and immediately set out to kill Humbaba together.

● When Humbaba died, he said that neither Gilgamesh nor Enkidu would live to old age. Enkidu did die soon after in another adventure, but in most versions of the poem, Gilgamesh doesn't die.

Gallu

WINGS
Because it was a
demon, a gallu
had wings.

CLAWS
People who knew that a gallu was coming to take them to
the underworld would try to hide. The gallu's clawlike
hands were especially useful in torturing people into telling
where other people were hiding.

HORNS
As a symbol that it was
working for the underworld,
a gallu had horns.

BRAINS
A gallu was not the
brightest demon, but it
didn't always have to be.
It acted as part of a gang
and took orders from the
underworld.

ARMS
A gallu needed very
strong arms because its
job was to drag people to
the underworld.

In Babylonian and Assyrian mythology, gallu (plural galla) was an underworld demon, who was said to carry victims to the underworld. The gallu could not be bribed, nor did it eat or drink. It didn't understand friendship or love. It would tear a child from its parents' arms if it was time to take the child to the underworld. Galla were bigger than most people and would appear as a gang on Earth, if necessary, attacking the person to take them down to the underworld. If someone tried to hide from them, the galla would hunt them down, torturing friends and family until they were told the hiding place.

ACTUAL SIZE

▶ WHEN INNANA IN THE UNDERWORLD learned that her husband Dumuzi was not mourning her death, she sent seven galla to fetch him. She would return to Earth and instead Dumuzi would be doomed to live in the underworld. Dumuzi twice managed to escape from the galla, but the third time they caught him. The first galla hit him with a nail on the cheek. The second hit him on the other cheek with a shepherd's hook. The other galla broke his milk churn and drinking cup. Then, they dragged him to the underworld.

Where in the world?

Across Mesopotamia. The galla are said to have taken Dumuzi to the underworld at Harran, now in southern Turkey.

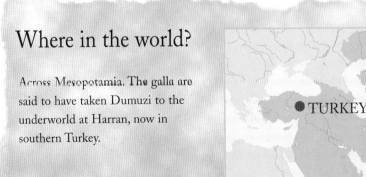

TURKEY

Did you know?

• Some versions say that if a lamb is sacrificed for a gallu, it stops hunting humans for a while.

• When Innana's father, the god Enki, discovered that she was in the underworld, he molded two galla demons of his own, Kurgarra and Galatura, out of the dirt under his fingernails. They were sent to the underworld to bring Innana back.

• To escape from the galla the first time, Dumuzi prayed to the gods. They turned his feet into those of a gazelle, enabling him to flee the galla very quickly.

• To save Dumuzi, his sister, Geshtinana, offered to spend six months of the year in the underworld. The months when Dumuzi, god of vegetation, was in the underworld began at the summer solstice on June 22nd, when the days start getting shorter.

Alecto

WINGS
Alecto had the wings of a bird or bat and flew all over Greece, carrying out her punishments on guilty people. This included cutting out the tongues of horses that dared to be human and speak.

BODY
Alecto carried a torch and, in desperate times, could inhabit the body of another woman if needed.

EYES
From her eyes oozed pus and she could drive a man insane with a simple look. But she was a calm spirit, not an angry one, and would punish other people's unjust anger.

HAIR
Alecto and the other Erinyes (furies) had snakes instead of hair.

This fierce beast is one of the Erinyes (furies) in Greek mythology. Alecto was born from drops of blood that fell to Earth from the great Titan, Uranus. She is responsible for war and revenge and punishes crimes, such as lying and murder, particularly murder within families. Her name means "unceasing anger." She can silence people and drive them crazy, yet is not crazy herself: if necessary, she will argue in court why someone should be driven insane by her. When the dead first arrive in Hades, the Underworld, the Erinyes purify the good of their sins but drag the wicked to the dungeon of the damned.

ACTUAL SIZE

▶ WHEN ALKMAION LEARNED THAT HIS MOTHER had been responsible for his father's death, he killed her. But Alkmaion's mother's Erinyes, including Alecto, pursued him and drove him insane. Alkmaion ran away, however, and was purified. He began a new life, but in spite of the purification, he was still poisoned and he ruined the crops. So, he left again and was told to go to a place where the sun hadn't shone when his crime had been committed. He found new land created from sand deposited on a riverbed, and made his home there.

Where in the world?

Athens, Greece. In a later tale Alecto and the Erinyes are renamed the "kindly goddesses" and are worshipped at the Acropolis in Athens.

●ATHENS

Did you know?

. . . .

● In Homer's epic poem *The Iliad*, a chariot-horse of Achilles, called Xanthos, speaks aloud to his master. Because it is unnatural for horses to speak, Alecto cut off the horse's tongue in punishment.

● In Virgil's epic poem *The Aeneid*, Alecto's mission is to stop the Trojan enemy. To do this, she takes over the body of the Latin queen, Amata, and calls for all Latin mothers to riot against the Trojans.

● Orestes's father had also been killed by his mother and Orestes, too, killed his mother in revenge. But, like Alkmaion, his mother's Erinyes drove him insane in punishment.

● It is uncertain how many Erinyes there were, but the most common number is three: Alecto, Megaera ("jealous one"), and Tisiphone ("avenging murder").

Vritra

BODY
Vritra was 4,500 miles (7,250 km) long and 1500 miles (2,415 km) wide. It was also known as Ahi, meaning "snake." Vritra was an Asura, a god who sought greater power.

STRENGTH
Twice Vritra managed to break Indra's jaw, but they fought on. Indra was king of the gods and god of storms, yet Vritra was the stronger of the two. Only through cunning could Indra beat Vritra.

HEAD
Vritra's head was big enough to swallow the Hindu god Indra completely. Luckily for Indra, the other gods forced Vritra to spit him out unharmed.

TAIL
Vritra's enormous body was used to block all the rivers of India, causing massive droughts.

Vritra was a fierce serpent created by Tvashtri, a brahmin (priest). Tvashtri wanted to overthrow Indra, the god of storms and war and one of the main gods in Hindu mythology. To do this, Tvashtri first created a son, Trisiras, who had three heads: one for reading scriptures; one for eating; and one for looking at the world. As the boy grew more religious and strong, Indra felt threatened. Finally, he sent a thunderbolt and killed the boy. But Tvashtri made Vritra to avenge his son's death. Vritra and Indra began a fierce battle, which Indra finally won, killing Vritra.

ACTUAL SIZE

▶ DURING THE BATTLE, VRITRA SWALLOWED INDRA. Horrified, the other gods made Vritra spit Indra out and the battle continued. Indra, though, wasn't strong enough to carry on and so he ran away. The god Vishnu made them stop fighting. Indra agreed he'd never attack Vritra with a weapon of wood, stone, or iron, nor with anything wet or dry, nor during the day or night. Then one sunset he saw a pillar of foam rising from sea. The foam was neither wood, nor stone nor metal, neither wet nor dry. He threw the pillar at Vritra and killed him.

Where in the world?

Northern India. Although the story is included in Hindu mythology, it originally came from the earlier Vedic religion (3500–3000 B.C.E).

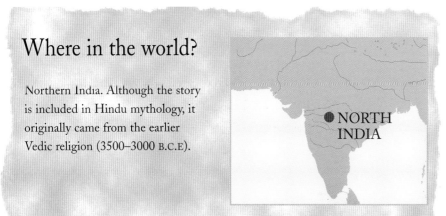

● NORTH INDIA

Did you know?

• Vritra was not only seen as a serpent but also as a dragon, a snake, and even a cloud.

• In the earlier Vedic version of the story, Vritra caused a drought across India. Vritra's name means "enveloper," because he closed off the waters. However, Indra, in defeating Vritra, released the waters again. In the battle, Vritra broke Indra's two jaws, but Indra knocked Vritra down and he fell on his own fortresses, crushing them.

• In the ancient Indian language Sanskrit, Vritra means "storm cloud." Indra originally means "strong," and his thunderbolt is said to have 100 edges.

• Indra freed life on Earth, but because he had killed the brahmin's son, he was forced into exile.

Camazotz

WINGS
Enormous batlike wings enable the camazotz to swoop in and attack at terrifying speeds and maneuver easily even in great swarms.

EARS
Like all bats, the camazotz relied on highly sensitive echolocation, which is like radar, to understand where things were in the dark.

TEETH
Its teeth were sharp enough to cut off a head in one swift bite.

TALONS
Like the teeth, these talons were sharp enough to slice off a head.

C amazotz were deadly, blood-sucking, batlike monsters with a nose like a knife. According to Mayan mythology, they lived in the underworld, known as Xibalba—the "place of fear"—which was ruled by the Mayan death gods. In Xibalba, there were six houses built to test the skills of people who were summoned there. These were the houses of darkness, razors, jaguars, bats, fire, and heat. Failing a test meant certain death. In some versions of the story, the camazotz was also a vampire god—half man and half bat, who would cut off a visitor's head with the talons on his feet.

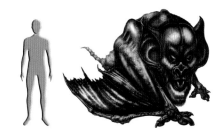

ACTUAL SIZE

▶ HAVING DISTURBED THE GODS WITH THEIR BALL GAME, Xbalanque and Hunahpu were challenged to survive a night in the Underworld bat house. All night, camazotz swarmed around, but the boys squeezed themselves into their blow pipes and stayed safe. In the morning, Hunahpu peeked out and a Camazotz swooped down and cut off his head. Delighted, the gods arranged to use Hunahpu's head as a ball. But Xbalanque made a new head out of a squash, returning the real head to Hunahpu. Then, the boys beat the gods at the ball game.

Where in the world?

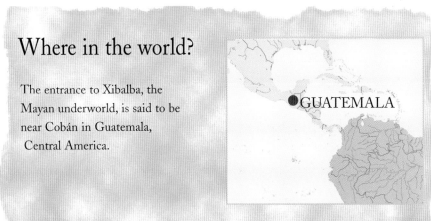

● GUATEMALA

The entrance to Xibalba, the Mayan underworld, is said to be near Cobán in Guatemala, Central America.

Did you know?

● Some people believe that the myth of the camazotz comes from the New World leaf-nosed bat, which has a nose similar to the knifelike nose described in the story.

● Camazotz means "death bat" in the Mayan K'iche' language, which is still spoken in Guatemala today.

● The story of the hero twins and camazotz was lost for many years and rediscovered only in 1701, when a Spanish priest in Guatemala found in his church the only manuscript of the *Popul Vuh*, the story of K'iche' myths and history.

● While still in Xibalba, Xbalanque cut Hunahpu in half and brought his brother back to life. This impressed the Xibalba gods and they demanded it be done to them. The boys killed the gods but, of course, didn't bring them back to life.

Argos

EYES
Even when he slept, at least one of the eyes stayed open. Some versions of the story say that Hermes finally made Argos close all of his eyes by singing him to sleep. Other versions say that he just told a lot of boring stories until Argos dozed off and each eye had closed.

VISION
Argos had 100 eyes in his head. He was known as "all-seeing Argos" because every direction was covered by four eyes.

HANDS
With his powerful hands, Argos wields an axe and cuts off the half woman, half serpent Echidna's head.

CLOTHES
Argos's clothes were made from the skin of a bull he had killed, which had been ravaging the land.

In Greek mythology, Argos is a 100-eyed giant. He is known as "all-seeing" because, even when he sleeps, one eye always remains open and awake. He is the goddess Hera's servant and is given the task of killing Echidna who, to the waist, is a beautiful woman, but has the tail of a terrible snake. She lives deep underground in a cave. Any men who see her pretty face but don't notice her vile tail until it is too late are dragged into the cave and killed. Argos waits at the mouth of the cave until Echidna is asleep and then rushes in and cuts off her head.

ACTUAL SIZE

▶ HERA ASKED ARGOS TO GUARD A COW. In reality, the cow was Io, a nymph whom Hera's husband, Zeus, king of the gods, was in love with. Zeus gave Hermes the task of rescuing Io. Hermes disguised himself as a shepherd and approached Argos. Hermes played his lyre and spoke spells to each of Argos's eyes, sending them to sleep. When Hermes was sure that Argos was asleep, he dropped a stone on Argos's head, killing him. When she found the body, Hera transferred Argos's eyes to the peacock's tail.

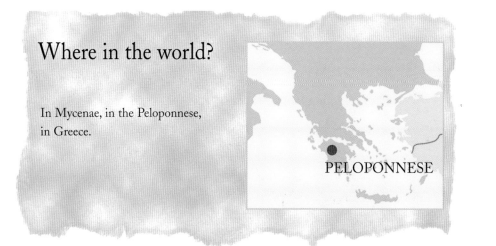

Where in the world?

In Mycenae, in the Peloponnese, in Greece.

PELOPONNESE

Did you know?

• Argos is also known as "Argos Panoptes," which means "All-eyes Argos."

• In revenge for Zeus freeing Io from Argos's captivity, Hera distracts Io with a fly, which leads her to wander all over Greece and farther and farther away from home, following the insect.

• In the Harry Potter novels, Argus Filch is the name of the caretaker at Hogwarts School of Witchcraft and Wizardry. He is known to be all-seeing.

• Argos was often seen wearing a bull skin, since he killed a bull that had ravaged the land. He also killed a satyr that had been robbing and murdering the people of King Apis of Argos, which is a city in the Peloponnese in Greece.

Atraoimen

TAIL
The atraoimen's powerful tail had such a mighty flick that it killed a few of its sons, sending them flying against trees on land and onto rocks in the sea.

FIN
The appearance of atraoimen's long fin at the surface of the water was often the first warning to one of its sons that the atraoimen had found him.

TEETH
The atraoimen caught the bait of one of its son's fishing rods and pulled him into the water, where it devoured him.

LEGS
The atraoimen was a sea monster, but it could walk a little and survive on land for a time. It hunted for some of its sons down in the caves along the shoreline.

This sea creature may look monstrous but inside is the soul of a good man, Kalinago, who was murdered. Kalinago left the mainland and settled on a Caribbean island. There, he had a happy life, married, and had many sons. However, his sons were jealous of their father's success so they used poison to kill him, and Kalinago's soul passed into the body of the atraoimen. Then, as the atraoimen, Kalinago hunted down his sons, who fled across the Caribbean. On each island, thinking they were safe, they settled and had families, but each time the atraoimen caught up with them. In this way, the Caribbean islands were populated.

ACTUAL SIZE

▶ TIMBE, ONE OF KALINAGO'S SONS, REACHED A NEW ISLAND. He thought he was now safe from his father. He killed the men on the island and set up the heads of the dead warriors to remind people of his success. He married a woman and they had a family. Timbe was out fishing one day when a fish took the bait and pulled so hard that Timbe fell into the water. Underwater, he saw the fish and realized that it was his father, as the atraoimen, who had come for him. The atraoimen devoured Timbe.

Where in the world?

In the Lesser Antilles Islands in the southeastern Caribbean. The Caribs migrated from northern South America to the Caribbean islands around 1200 C.E.

SOUTHEAST CARIBBEAN

Did you know?

● The Caribbean people also tell the story of Bakwa, a snake-king that left the sea and sleeps in the hills. It will come back to the people when they are at peace.

● Before the Carib people lived in the Caribbean, Taino people had already arrived there from South America.

● Another Caribbean sea monster is the lusca. It might be a gigantic octopus, much larger than the normal largest octopus and said to grow 220 feet (67 m) long.

● In 1896 in Florida, a mass of unidentified rotting sea creature was washed ashore. This was given the name St. Augustine's Monster. It has never been properly identified, but recent theories suggest that it was part of a rotting sperm whale.

Morrigan

ABILITY TO FLY
Morrigan appeared to soldiers about to enter battle as a crow flying overhead. To some, she gave encouragement, but to others her presence brought fear, causing them to lose the battle.

CROW
If Morrigan landed as a crow on the shoulder of a soldier, it meant that the gods had decided it was his time to die. He would lose his strength and his enemies could be confident about attacking him.

HANDS
Morrigan also appeared as "The Washer at the Ford." If she washed a soldier's armor before he went into battle, it meant he was going to die fighting.

SHAPE
Morrigan was a shape-shifter. To Cú Chulainn she appeared as a beautiful young woman, but when he rejected her, she shifted into a deadly eel and attacked him.

In the Celtic mythology of Ireland, the goddess of war, Morrigan, could change her shape, becoming both different humans (a beautiful young woman, an old milkmaid) and different animals (most often a raven or a crow). Usually, she did not fight herself but influenced the minds of the soldiers. Her appearance alone could scare soldiers who were about to enter battle, and she could easily change innocent people into pools of water. Morrigan means "queen of the ghosts" and she was also goddess of the underworld. She foresaw the death of the Irish warrior hero Cú Chulainn, telling him: "I guard your death."

ACTUAL SIZE

▶ MORRIGAN FIRST APPEARED TO CÚ CHULAINN (pronounced koo-kull-in) as a beautiful woman, but he rejected her love. In revenge, she appeared as a deadly eel, but Cú Chulainn wounded her. Then, she appeared as a wolf and Cú Chulainn poked out her eye. Next, she appeared as a cow, but Cú Chulainn broke her leg. Finally, she appeared as an old woman milking a cow. She offered Cú Chulainn milk, but he didn't recognize her, and gave her his blessings. At that moment, her battle wounds healed and she and Cú Chulainn made peace.

Where in the world?

Morrigan was often described as living in the cave of Cruachain in County Roscommon, Ireland.

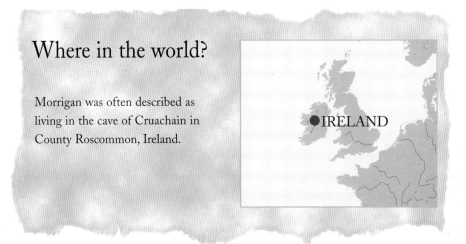

●IRELAND

Did you know?

● Cú Chulainn tied himself upright to a rock with his own intestines so that he could die upright. Morrigan appeared as a crow and landed on his shoulder. This meant that it was safe for Cú Chulainn's enemies to approach him and cut off his head. Cú Chulainn was then killed by a spear.

● Morrigan was also a prophetess and warned the Brown Bull of Cuailnge what would happen in the war between the Irish counties of Connacht and Ulster.

● Morrigan and Cú Chulainn first appear in manuscripts from the Ulster Cycle, Irish legends and sagas collected from the 12th to the 15th centuries. However, the stories themselves are probably as old as the seventh century.

● Morrigan's son Mechi had three hearts, each with a serpent in it. He would have caused disaster for Ireland, but the warrior Mac Cécht killed Mechi and burned his body.

Xingtian

AXE
In a duel with the Yellow Emperor, Xingtian lost his head, but he fought blindly on with his axe and shield.

LEGS
Despite losing his head, Xingtian was not discouraged and he kept up a war dance. He has become a symbol in China for staying determined even when things go very wrong.

FACE
After his head had been cut off, the giant Xingtian tried to make a face on his chest. He wanted to use his nipples for eyes and his navel for a mouth, but his "eyes" couldn't see and his "mouth" wouldn't open.

Xingtian may have become a horrible headless blind beast, but even for a giant he once held a more respected position. He had been an official with Emperor Yan and later fought with the six-armed, four-eyed Chi You against the Yellow Emperor. But when the Yellow Emperor defeated Chi You, Xingtian demanded a duel. During the duel the Yellow Emperor cut off Xingtian's head, which was buried inside Changyang Mountain. But despite this, Xingtian's body didn't die, and it fought on, headless. He tried using his navel for a mouth and his nipples for eyes, but his mouth didn't open and his eyes couldn't see.

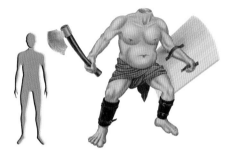

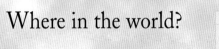

ACTUAL SIZE

▶ THE YELLOW EMPEROR ACCEPTED XINGTIAN'S CHALLENGE to a duel and the two fought ferociously, the emperor's sword battling against Xingtian's axe. The emperor managed to distract the giant and cut off Xingtian's head. But as it rolled across the ground, the head kept roaring and Xingtian's body kept blindly trying to catch hold of it. The head rolled toward the foot of Changyang Mountain. The Yellow Emperor struck the mountain with his sword, the mountain split open, and Xingtian's head rolled inside. Then, the mountain closed up and Xingtian's head was never seen again.

Where in the world?

Changyang Mountain (Eternally Auspicious Mountain), China. The story dates from before 220 B.C.E.

●CHINA

Did you know?

• Xingtian celebrated his survival by performing a dance with an axe and his shield. Despite being defeated and losing his head, he fought on. He symbolizes someone whose spirit is never crushed.

• A version of the Xingtian story appears in the *Shan Hai Jing* (*Collection of the Mountains and Seas*). It's a compilation of early Chinese texts on geography and mythology written between the fourth to the second century B.C.E.

• Xingtian's name means "punished one" or "he who was punished by heaven."

• There are other tales of headless beasts. In medieval Europe, they were known as Blemmyes and were believed to live in Africa. Among the Navajo in North America there was Theelgeth.

Xiang Yao

HEADS
With nine human heads, the giant serpent Xiang Yao could eat from nine different mountaintops at the same time.

ARMS
Xiang Yao's giant arms reached far out, pulling up trees, knocking down houses, and diverting rivers.

BODY
When Xiang Yao was wounded, the blood that spurted from his wounds smelled foul and poisoned the land. The warrior Zhu Rong dug the soil out three times to make it good again for farming, but each time the blood just sank in more deeply.

TAIL
Xiang Yao's tail churned up the countryside and blocked rivers, spoiling crops, causing an enormous stink, and polluting freshwater.

Xiang Yao was a serpent whose nine heads ate from nine different mountains. He accompanied the water dragon, Gong Gong, in polluting the land across China. Frustrated with his minor job running errands in the court of heaven, Gong Gong rebelled against the emperor. Together, Xiang Yao and Gong Gong dammed up rivers and created thunderclouds, bringing terrible floods and polluting more land. They enjoying killing people, but could not overthrow the powers of heaven. In battle, Xiang Yao was killed, but the blood that spurted from his wounds smelled foul and no crops would grow on any ground contaminated by it.

ACTUAL SIZE

▶ XIANG YAO AND GONG GONG BATTLED FOR DAYS across the heavens against Zhu Rong, the god of fire, who rode an enormous tiger. But they could not defeat Zhu Rong. In anger, Gong Gong threw himself into Mount Buzhou, a mountain that held up the heavens. Then, the heavens opened and an even greater catastrophe followed as fire and flood swept the Earth. All kinds of terrible creatures came from the heavens, ruining crops, killing people, and bringing plague. Xiang Yao was killed by Zhu Rong, while the creator goddess Nüwa repaired the heavens.

Where in the world?

It is thought the mythical Mount Buzhou is in the Pamir Mountains in the far west of China.

●WEST CHINA

Did you know?

• When he ran into the mountain, Gong Gong tilted the heavens and Earth, which is why, according to the myth, the sun, moon, and stars move to the west and why all rivers in China flow east.

• The goddess Nüwa, who is part human and part dragon, repaired the heavens by cutting off the legs of the giant tortoise Ao, using them to prop up the heavens.

• In some versions of the story, Gong Gong is Zhu Rong's son and he isn't killed but sulks away in shame after being defeated. In another version, the goddess Nüwa kills Xiang Yao.

• The story of Xiang Yao is one of China's creation myths about how the world came to be. In Chinese mythology the oldest character is Pangu, a hairy giant, who created the world with his axe by separating the Earth from the Sky.

Index

Aladdin 38–39
Alecto 80–81
The Alps 29
Amarok 20–21
Amine 9
Ammut 74–75
anaye (alien gods) 71
Andersen, Hans Christian 63
Anubis 75
Arabia 9
Argos 86–87
Atraoimen 88–89
Australia 31

Baba Yaga 10–11
Baldr 67
Balkans 15
banshees 33
Barsoom (Mars) 60, 61
Basile, Giambattista 51
basilisk 23
Bilbo Baggins 17, 55
blemyahs 71
bunyips 30–31
Burroughs, Edgar Rice 61

The Call of Cthulhu
    (Lovecraft) 65
camazotz 84–85
Canada 21
Caribbean islands 89
Carter, John 61
China 39, 92, 93, 95
The Chronicles of Narnia
    (Lewis) 63
Chudo-Yudo 11
cockatrice 22–23
Cthulhu 64–65
Czech Republic 49

Denmark 13, 17
Dracula (Stoker) 45

dragons
    Chudo-Yudo 11
    cockatrice 22–23
    Humbaba 76–77
    Zmag Oghjeni Vuk 14–15
Dumuzi 79

Echidna 86, 87
Erinyes (furies) 80, 81
Egypt 73, 75
the elf king 12–13
The Emperor's New Clothes
    (Andersen) 63
England
    cockatrice 23
    the giant from Jack and the
        Beanstalk 43
    Lambton Worm 45
    red weed 57
    the wolf from The Three
        Little Pigs 41
Enkidu 76, 77
Erben, K.J. 49

Fenrir 67, 69
The Flea 51
Fredon 35

gallu 78–79
Gandalf 17, 58, 59
genies 39
Germany 13
ghouls 8–9
the giant from Jack and the
    Beanstalk 42–43
the giant from Sinbad's Third
    Voyage 36–37
giants
    Argos 86–87
    the giant from Jack and the
        Beanstalk 42–43
    the giant from Sinbad's

Third Voyage 36–37
    Humbaba 76–77
    the ogre from The Flea
        50–51
    Polyphemus 37
    Xingtian 92–93
Gilgamesh 76, 77
goblins 24–25
Gollum 54–55
Gong Gong 95
Greece 25, 81, 87
Greedy Guts (Otesanek) 49
Greenland 21
Guatemala 85

Hermes 86, 87
The Hobbit (Tolkien) 16, 17,
    55
Hogwarts School 53, 87
Horus 73
Humbaba 76–77

India 27, 83
Indra 82, 83
Innana 79
Iran 35, 77
Iraq 37
Ireland 91
Isis 73
Italy 51

Jack and the Beanstalk 42–43
Japan 47
John Carter of Mars
    (Burroughs) 61
Jormungand 67, 68–69

Kachi-Kachi Yama 47
Kai 62, 63
Kalinago 89
kallikantzaros 24–25
Kallo and the Goblins 25

King Lear (Shakespeare) 43
Koshei the Deathless 11

The Lair of the White Worm
    (Stoker) 45
Lambton Worm 44–5
langsuirs 32–3
Lewis, C.S. 63
The Little Mermaid
    (Andersen) 63
Little Otik 48–9
Little Shop of Horrors 49
Loki 66–7, 68, 69
The Lord of the Rings
    (Tolkien) 55, 58, 59
Lovecraft, H.P. 65

Malaysia 33
Medusa 23
Mesopotamia 77, 79
Morrigan 90–1

Navajo people 70, 71
Nayanezgani 71
Nuckelavee 18–19
Nüwa 95

Odin 68
Odysseus 37
the ogre from The Flea 50–1
orcs 59
Osiris 73, 75

Peer Gynt (Ibsen) 17
Polyphemus 37
pontianaks 33
Popul Vuh 85
Potter, Harry 9, 53, 87

Ragnarök 67, 69
red weed 56–7
Rowling, J.K. 53

Russia 11

Saruman 58–59
Sauron 59
Scandinavia
    the elf king 13
    Jormungand 69
    Loki 67
    trolls 17
Scotland 19, 53
Set 72–73
Shakespeare, William 43
Shrek 41
Sidi Numan 9
Sinbad 36–37
The Snow Queen 62–63
the sorcerer from Aladdin
    38–39
South Pacific 65
Spitzbergen 63
Stoker, Bram 45

The Tale of Tales (Il
    Pentamerone) (Basile) 51
Tales from Bohemia (Erben)
    49
tanuki 46–47
tatzelwurm 28–29
Tharks 60–61
Theelgeth 70–71
Thobadzistshini 71
Thor 67, 68, 69
A Thousand and One Nights
    9, 37, 39
The Three Little Pigs 41
Tolkien, J.R.R. 16, 17, 55, 59
trolls 16–17

The Ugly Duckling
    (Andersen) 63
the underworld 73, 75, 78,
    79, 81, 85

United States 61, 71

Vetala 26–27
Vikram, King 27
Voldemort, Lord 52–53
Vritra 82–83
Vsleslav, Prince of Polotsk 15
Vuk Gregurevic Brankovic 15

The War of the Worlds
    (Wells) 56–7
Wells, H.G. 56–57
werewolves 14–15
The White Witch 63
witches
    Baba Yaga 10–11
    The White Witch 63
wolves
    Amarok 20–21
    Fenrir 67, 69
    the wolf from The Three
        Little Pigs 40–41
worms
    Lambton Worm 44–45
    tatzelwurm 28–29

Xiang Yao 94–95
Xingtian 92–93

Yellow Emperor 92, 93

Zahhak 34–35
Zeus 87
Zhu Rong 94, 95
Zmag Oghjeni Vuk 14–15